The Politics of Appalachian Rhetoric

THE POLITICS OF APPALACHIAN RHETORIC

—

Amanda E. Hayes

WEST VIRGINIA UNIVERSITY PRESS
MORGANTOWN 2018

Copyright 2018 West Virginia University Press
First edition published 2018 by West Virginia University Press
Printed in the United States of America

ISBN:
Cloth 978-1-946684-45-5
Paper 978-1-946684-46-2
Ebook 978-1-946684-47-9

Library of Congress Cataloging-in-Publication Data is available from the
Library of Congress

Cover design by Than Saffel / WVU Press

Contents

ACKNOWLEDGEMENTS

If books grow from places, mine sprouts from a few. The first is a farm in the Ohio hills and the people who have lived there, past and present. The more recent generations I have to thank include my aunts, uncles, and cousins. I especially thank my grandparents: my Grandma and Pap, who did more for me than I could express, and my Grandma Hayes, from whom I inherited my eyes and my love of reading. My brother, who is our whole family's unpaid but highly deserving tech support, and my parents: my mother, who supported this project from the start and who helped me think through so much of *how* we think, and my father, whose hard work put me through college in the first place.

The second place that helped grow this book is college, where I discovered the books and voices that made me consider rhetoric at all. The first is Ohio University's Eastern campus, where I learned to love school more than I thought possible. Thank you to all the dedicated faculty there, especially Dr. Tom Flynn and the late Dr. David Noble, and my fellow English major Sara McKinnon, for sitting me down at her kitchen table and helping me fill out grad school applications when I was ready to give up. Thank you to the rhet-comp faculty at Ohio University, who never gave up on me, the quiet girl in their classes who never talked until after she'd heard everyone else and made up her own mind. Dr. Mara Holt has been my academic mom from the start, shepherding me through processes and program requirements that I would never even have been aware of on my own. I was lucky to find in her a teacher who demonstrates so well how rhetoric, composition, and teaching can matter outside the classroom door—it can have meaning for our entire world. Dr. Sherrie Gradin introduced me to rhetorical history beyond the Greco-Roman tradition and taught me to reconsider what rhetoric could be; without that, this book never would have gotten off the ground. Dr. Jennie Nelson has had an unwavering faith in me and my voice, more than I had in myself at times. Her supportive emails have kept me going through the revision and publication process. And thank you to Dr. Theodore Hutchinson, for supporting my dissertation research and introducing me to the work of Victoria Purcell-Gates.

For the peoples and places of Appalachia, I have more thank-yous than I could possibly put into words.

Introduction

Writing Takes Place

When I started writing what turned into this book, I was trying to answer a simple question. In his 2000 article "Rhetorical Sovereignty: What Do American Indians Want from Writing?" Scott Richard Lyons argued that what American Indian students want is rhetorical sovereignty: to have a voice in the language and rhetoric of classroom instruction. Gaining this voice in the classroom, he proposed, was a small but important step to achieving wider cultural rhetorical sovereignties; in other words, to attain the acknowledged right to name their own cultural identities and have that naming respected.

What Lyons's article gave me, in addition to the question itself, was a curiosity about its possible applications. At the bottom of the article, among my other copious notes, I wrote, *What do I, as an Appalachian, want from writing instruction? From writing?* Since then, my interests have moved beyond writing alone and into wider questions of rhetoric, by which I mean the concepts and styles of communication that were taken for granted in my regional upbringing. How do we write, if we write at all? What rhetorical assumptions do we bring to writing, and where do these come from? This book is my attempt to not only answer these questions, but to consider both why I draw the conclusions I do and what I believe shapes those conclusions. Of course, I can't answer these questions for all Appalachians, in part because Appalachia is so *much*. It is many peoples, many hilltops and hollers, towns and cities, many cultures, many variations. I can, however, consider it for myself, and I can offer my understanding and experience as a potential lens through which other Appalachian students, teachers, and administrators can view their own educational expectations and outcomes. And I can say that my experience with writing and writing instruction is one I've witnessed in my students and the students of colleagues: confusion, even in times of success and certainly in times of failure, about how we are meant to write and why, a sense of oddness or uneasiness about the conventions we are meant to follow. Why does academic writing seem strange to me, even now? What do I want from writing? What do I want it to do for me and my family, and how do I want our children to encounter it in the classroom?

Many writers and scholars have influenced the ways that both teachers and students think about cultural rhetorics and their sometimes *very* different appearance from the academic rhetorics encountered in the writing classroom. I hope to add to this body of knowledge because in order to think about what I, and perhaps other Appalachians, might want from writing and our rhetorical educations, I needed to think about what I brought with me from outside the classroom. What, in other words, shaped my methods and means of communication among family, friends, and neighbors, and how did it vary from what I encountered in my textbooks?

Using the cultural history of my particular region of Appalachian Ohio as a starting point, I sought to understand what affect this history could have on the ways writing, and to a degree communication itself, happens. Because regional immigration stemmed in large part from the Scotch-Irish, I wanted to see if any influence remained visible. While a great deal of research, particularly from linguist Michael Montgomery, has shown that the Scotch-Irish had an enduring linguistic effect on Appalachian dialect, particularly in the Central Appalachian region, I wanted to know if there might be something even deeper than that. In other words, does this heritage influence not just words but what gets communicated about and how? And, I discovered, it does.

What I'm doing in this book, then, is unraveling and examining a particular thread in the history of Appalachian rhetoric and expression, the aspect of it that has most greatly impacted my life and perspective. I had hoped to invite readers from other parts of the Appalachian region to look for possible commonalities within this examination, around which we could make a stronger united case for our right to rhetorical sovereignty: the right to decide for ourselves, as Appalachian peoples, how to make our own writing and rhetorical choices and to have those choices respected. I don't and never have claimed that Appalachian rhetoric has only one origin, nor that we within the region need to have Scotch-Irish descent in order to recognize and reclaim this form of expression. I look at the rhetoric I'm examining as being based in region rather than bloodline. However, it can be easy to miss or reject commonalities across groups or even sub-regions. I can see some readers, even those who consider themselves Appalachian, possibly feeling disconnected from my experience based on whether they hail from northern (as I do) or southern Appalachia, as we as a nation tend to see northern and southern identity as significantly different. They might see my project as an attempt to generalize Appalachian rhetoric and identity.

In fact, I have no interest in generalizing or simplifying any identity; in fact, I'd love to see *more* acknowledgement of the complexities inherent in Appalachian identity. What I am doing, however, is something I've learned to do in my own rhetorical upbringing: I'm seeking to create connections. I've lost count (actually, by the time I realized this was regionally unique, I hadn't even thought to start counting) of the conversations I've had with strangers in southeastern Ohio that involve a rundown of family surnames or previous addresses. "Are you related to any _____ or

_____?" I've heard asked over and over as strangers—people in the checkout line, viewers along a parade route, or riders on the bus—establish their connections to one other. Alternatively, I hear "Have you ever lived around _____?" If we aren't linked by blood, perhaps we are by place. It is not the links themselves that matter to me just now, it's the inclination to forge them that guided me in composing my sense of Appalachian rhetoric. *This is what it's like for me*, I hoped to ask. *Is it like this for you? What does it mean for us if it is?*

My research into Appalachian writing leads me to believe that there are aspects of this rhetorical tradition that weave beyond northern Appalachia. Regardless, in the interest of establishing my terms, I'll specify: I am northern Appalachian. Some of the primary texts I've researched for this book are by northern Appalachian, rural authors. Our shared background influences our voices, but also to a degree encourages our individuality. As Shenandoah University professor Warren Hofstra notes, "understanding individualism is critical"[1] to understanding Scotch-Irish culture, and one of the ways I've seen this value at play in my local rhetoric is a value for sharing ideas, but an unwillingness to force those ideas on others.

Which brings me to another disclaimer: this book is not a traditional academic argument. I never intended it to be. I worry that argument has become a sort of sickness in academic culture, or at least an addiction. Since when can we only learn from arguments? As a matter of fact, many of the arguments I encounter on a daily basis are more likely to shut down learning than to encourage it. While, again, fully allowing for variance in individual experiences, I've learned far more from people's stories than I have from their arguments. And I've never laid awake at night worried that my students didn't know how to argue. Rather, I've worried that they're forgetting how to listen. In my experience, social conditioning allows a story to encourage listening in ways an argument simply doesn't. To say that there is only one right way, the way of the academy, to write about Appalachian rhetoric is to miss the entire point of what makes Appalachian rhetoric potentially powerful.

Yet the way that many Appalachian writers tell their stories, employ their rhetoric, in the classroom remains under-recognized. What I'm doing in this work is, in part, demonstrating what I learned growing up in an Appalachian rhetorical culture: making my points not through argument but through story, through demonstration of my experience and thinking.

The rhetoric I'm working with doesn't take the form of a traditional academic argument. Because I'm working with rhetorical conventions outside of academic norms, the results might be confusing for readers who are conditioned to expect certain things from texts. For example, some of my chapters lack solid thesis statements, or if they have them, don't get around to making them until late. *This is a way of writing that is rhetorical and culturally influenced.* In my experience, people don't preface their stories with a thesis nor do they insist on one interpretation of what they have to say. They don't focus exclusively on audience expectations; they tell stories to solidify their own thinking as much as, or more than, to convince someone else to agree with it. I grew up believing I, and everyone else, had the right to "speak their piece"; I might well change my mind based on someone else's story . . . and then again, I might not. But the more someone tries to insist I change it, the less likely that outcome is. And, based on my experience and Kim Donehower's examination of residents in Kanawha County, West Virginia, I don't think that stubbornness is just an individual quirk. I think it's connected to the rhetorical conditions in which I grew up and which I am examining in this book.

So why write about Appalachian rhetoric? It's a question that could just as easily be applied to any form of cultural rhetoric: because it adds to our field of knowledge. Also, I do it because the field of rhetoric and composition is becoming increasingly interested in the influence of place-based dynamics on writing, and the rhetorical tradition I describe can add to that discussion. I want to say something about how writing instruction can work in a marginalized culture, how it can work *for* us rather than at odd with us. And finally because, in the wake of the 2016 election cycle, Appalachian cultures and values are becoming more puzzling and seemingly out of step than ever. Who are these people, and why don't they make any sense? Why do they vote against their own interests? These are both questions I've encountered more than once. They are questions I'm not sure many of us within the region have really had the chance to ponder, either.

Yet recently, I've noticed ripples of a "fine, forget Appalachia, let them reap what they sow" attitude, among both regional and nonregional people of my acquaintance. I understand the frustration because I too have watched my neighbors vote for the people who seem most eager to exploit us and rewind any social progress our country has made. But I also think the "forget them, they obviously want to suffer, leave them to their own devices, who cares if we understand each other or not" concept is flawed. For one thing, it assumes such a separation between "Appalachia" and "not Appalachia" is possible; the recent election, however, demonstrated that what Appalachia thinks is indeed relevant to other Americans because it plays a role in who leads this country. This attitude also essentializes Appalachian identity and culture—it assumes that we are all one thing and think one way, a way that is racist, sexist, homophobic, and anti-immigrant. It's a concept that erases the many, many Appalachians who don't fit that profile, including those who are part of ethnic minority groups, are LGBTQI, and/or are immigrants. It also doubts the very possibility of education and empathy within the region. If we as Appalachians are all so set in our ways, so separate, so ingrained in our prejudices, and so unwilling to listen to anyone whom those prejudices deem to be "other," then there's no hope for us anyway. Such a view more or less states that there are simply some (non-Appalachian) people who are strong enough and wise enough to see from other people's perspectives, even when those perspectives challenge their own beliefs, and then there are the many others, who are not. It is time, according to this view, for the wise to stop babying the weak and self-centered and somehow just "get on with it" (whatever it is) without them. I suppose the "it" is the moral betterment of society. Except that, as a means of making society better, of making the oppressed and marginalized more heard and more free, this attitude seems pretty counterproductive. If we give up on trying to listen to people across difference, then how does social change and growth even happen?

I'm writing about Appalachian rhetoric, then, because I don't want any of us to stop trying to listen. But listening requires that we tell our stories, and understanding requires that we tell them the ways they want and need to be told. What I'm trying to do is write about my rhetorical culture in a way that feels authentic to it. It's an approach to writing that we aren't used to seeing in the academy, at least usually not outside developmental writing classes, and that has, as I've noted, created questions and even consternation. Readers of texts written in the ways I describe might find these works frustrating or even poorly composed. "You keep jumping back and forth between academic prose and personal anecdote, and I don't understand why," I've been told. At least now, *I* understand why I wrote in these ways—because both were part of me, part of my rhetoric, and both carried equal weight. One of the points I raise about the Appalachian rhetoric I'm describing is that it is, essentially, writer-focused rather than reader-focused. While I'm not intentionally trying to confuse the reader, I am trying to demonstrate what makes sense for me—how my personal, linguistic, and literary experiences have come together to create a meaning that I find valuable and worth sharing. The result may not be the most conventional read, especially for those conditioned to expect an A to B to C chronology in writing. And yet, everything in this book is here because it has meaning for me.

My purpose in writing this way is simple: it is a way of writing that feels right, and it is how many regional students come to the classroom writing. They may or may not know that it *is* a way of writing—of not only expressing, but also creating one's ideas and values—that doesn't fit the academic norm. They may or may not know that the ways of writing that feel natural to them can stem from the historical and cultural conditions they've grown up in. (In fact, I think that, particularly in northern Appalachia, they *don't* know this, specifically because Appalachian identity or heritage isn't something frequently discussed in our schools). And what neither teachers nor students might know is that this style of writing is richly rhetorical—it functions in particular ways, for particular reasons, that I'm trying to demonstrate and explain in this book.

This leads me to another potential area of concern—who exactly those readers ought to be. Again, my initial response to this query is a hesitation, born I believe from my connection-seeking rhetorical background: why the need to delineate an audience? Why not just say that I'm writing this for whoever might find value in it—Appalachian or non-Appalachian, teacher or student? However, I will say this: I hope that any readers who are students, particularly if they're from areas in northern Appalachia that are, at least in my experience, less likely to encounter discussions of regional identities in schools, will come away understanding why the types of writing they're asked to do might not come "naturally." It isn't because you are stupid, it isn't because you can't write. Perhaps it's simply a matter of belonging to a rhetorical system influenced by a heritage different than the roots of traditional academic discourse. I hope that any readers who are teachers, particularly if they teach within the region, will understand more of where their students might be coming from, regionally and rhetorically, and be even more willing to approach these backgrounds with respect. And I hope, for any reader, that this book contributes something to their understanding of the rich cultural quilt that is rhetoric in the United States.

———

What is rhetoric? The answer, I've come to discover, depends on who you ask. Some will argue that rhetoric is, at its most basic, just that: argument. The available means of persuasion. If that's true, then the people I grew up with in Appalachian Ohio and northern West Virginia are the least rhetorical people I know. They argue, of course. I've heard plenty of people tell someone else that "you're wrong, I'm right, here's why," in a variety of tones. But arguing as a means of persuasion? I'm not sure I can name one time when someone I know actually argued someone else into changing their minds about anything.

My definition of rhetoric, then, particularly in terms of my regional background, is something more nuanced. In my experience, when people really want to say—or write—something important, they tell a story. Specifically, they tell the story of how they have come to believe or decide something. Listening to how others decide what matters is, I believe, a deeply rhetorical act. Rhetoric is, for the purposes I'm examining in this book, how we tell and use our stories and the stories of those around us to decide who we are and what we stand for. Thus, telling our stories can be the way we solidify knowledge for ourselves. Because who we are and what we think is, in itself, rhetorical, we shape the people around us with every casual encounter. The telling of a story can be how we create and share what matters to us, softly. A story is an invitation, not an insistence. Whether you come away agreeing or not . . . that's really up to you. Or maybe it will stew awhile; you'll carry it around, tucked away, until you find it influencing your beliefs in ways you never imagined. Or maybe hearing someone else's stories will simply get you to thinking about your own.

So let me tell you a story about why I'm writing this book the way I am. My Great-Grandma Carpenter was a master quilter. She didn't need a sewing machine; she pieced every one of her quilts by hand. I remember watching her quilt; I was pretty young at the time, but I knew quilting was something I wanted to do, too. Unfortunately, I was too young to have much patience. The stitches had to be so small and so exact . . . I managed to knot up the thread a few stitches into my one and only solo effort and gave up the entire enterprise. It's up in my grandparents' attic now, that little piece of batted cotton I was too impatient to quilt when I was five. It's in the cedar chest, just like some of Grandma Carpenter's quilts are. I wonder if somebody knew better than I did at the time how much I'd regret giving up. I did learn to crochet eventually, taught by the mother of one of my grade school classmates. But it wasn't the same. Crochet, unlike quilting, wasn't part of the family.

We in the family don't need any other reason to love Grandma Carpenter's quilts but that they were made by her. Still, it wasn't until within the last few years that I learned to see those quilts in a new light, as something precious not just because of the messages of love and artistry that they'd always conveyed for me. In fact, I've only recently been learning to read them and to read quilting as a whole as something even more deeply rhetorical than I'd ever realized. The realization tracks directly to my discovery of Fawn Valentine's *West Virginia Quilts and Quiltmakers*, wherein she explores the cultural roots of Appalachian quilting. She explains ways of reading the cultural traditions of quilts through their designs and constructions. For example, Scotch-Irish-influenced quilts regularly consisted of a traditional pattern, such as a star-burst or rings, but within that pattern could lay a chaos of apparently unrelated colors and cloth configurations. The whole was over-layered by a pattern of intersecting, often wave-like stitching, giving the quilt an equal sense of order and chaos, of circular and interlaced connections. Materials ("piece-goods" Grandma Carpenter called them) were often chosen for sentimental or value-laden reasons; a scrap of a quilter's wedding dress might be entwined with pieces of the blankets that swaddled each of her babies. Thus, what might at first glance appear a disorganized mishmash of clashing colors was actually an ode to the passages of a person's life.

I've come to think of this quilting as a system of communicating that privileges descriptive narrative (each piece of the quilt is an opening to an interconnected body of stories) and proposes as an end-goal the drawing of connections between consistency (in the traditional patterns) and difference (in the individualized structure) to create a whole text, a text that speaks of the quilter perhaps more than it speaks to the viewer. The resulting quilts require a sense of cultural literacy for best interpretation, as they require the willingness of the viewer/listener/interpreter to see the quilt as more than an object, to look at it as a cultural insider might, and to consider meanings beyond the surface materials. The color and cloth choices may seem clashing or chaotic to a viewer, in other words, but we have to realize that for the quilter, they have meaning, purpose. A quilt tells a story, but on its own subjective terms.

It is this sort of rhetorical literacy, a literacy that is needed to accept and understand my experience of Appalachian rhetoric, that my project hopes to advance. I don't know the stories behind Grandma Carpenter's quilts exactly, in that I don't know, and can no longer ask, why she chose the fabrics that she did, or why she placed one particular piece next to another. One quilt she made, for example, is made up of haphazardly arranged rectangles of patterned, multicolored cloth, surrounded by a bright red border and blue backing. Did these cloths or colors mean anything to her? Maybe the point in them wasn't necessarily to transmit specific stories to me, but to recollect them for herself; as Amy D. Clark describes Appalachian quilters, "They quilt . . . to remember."[2] I can't know the remembrances Grandma Carpenter wrote into her quilt, but I can learn from her example that *the act of remembering is important.* I imagine I've come to understand better now why she quilted at all, why she took the time and patience with those small and precise stitches, what she meant in doing it, and what it can mean for me and for others. If the quilt, and the quilting, are rhetorical products and acts, they are emblematic ones, grown from and created by a rhetorical tradition that I have perhaps performed myself without knowing I was doing it. But I want to know now. I want to quilt.

If I've learned anything, it's that the ways of thinking, speaking, writing, and valuing that I grew up with are easily misunderstood in academia as a whole. If, for example, when I was in school, I tried to compose an argumentative essay not via a thesis and topic sentences, but rather through a story I'd heard from my grandmother, I wasn't demonstrating a culturally based rhetorical approach; I was simply doing the assignment wrong. ("You don't want to tell a story here," a teacher told me once. "You want data to support a thesis." I was powerless at the time to question whether my story couldn't do both.) It's a misunderstanding I took to my own early work as a writing teacher.

This book examines my understandings and misunderstandings via a process of rhetorical analysis and self-interrogation. Ultimately, my chapters are organized based on the process of my thinking as I worked through my initial question, a system of organization that fits the style of rhetoric I describe. Because my project has two conjoined purposes—to examine an Appalachian rhetoric and to demonstrate it—my first chapter models how ethos might be established in that rhetoric. To do this, I present my context, foregrounding my place-connections and family history. Doing this demonstrates that I value these things, which is something an Appalachian audience may well recognize and identity with. The second chapter moves into a facet of Appalachian rhetoric that can either unite or divide Appalachian audiences: language. Despite stereotypes, not all Appalachian peoples share, or even value, their dialects. However, the visibility of language differences makes dialect perhaps the most well-trodden aspect of Appalachian identity. For those who don't share what might be called the "standard" Appalachian dialect, claiming that identity may feel more complicated than for others.

Because of this, I want to look at rhetoric as something that encapsulates more than language—it is also the process and means by which identity and values are shaped and conveyed. Chapter 3, therefore, looks at what the Appalachian rhetoric of my own upbringing entailed; specifically, I look for its roots in a Celtic rhetorical system transferred to the region by groups of Scotch-Irish immigrants. While this chapter considers what Celtic rhetoric looked and sounded like, Chapter 4 begins to examine its survival in the rural Appalachian region of my birth. Because my interests are specifically in writing and how people conceive of and use it, Chapter 5 looks at examples of texts written by Appalachian writers from my region. I consider how the types of writing these authors take part in actually utilize aspects of Celtic rhetoric, which may not be recognized *as* rhetoric either by their audiences or the authors themselves.

This potential lack of recognition forms the basis of the following chapter. I wanted to investigate why many Appalachian students, myself included, haven't learned about regional rhetorics or identity issues in their school experiences. Much of the reasoning, I posit, revolves around a lingering deficit ideology regarding Appalachian culture. How this deficit ideology influences what writing instruction looks like in many Appalachian classrooms is the focus of Chapter 7. In other words, ideas about what "good" writing is and what education should do for Appalachian students can work against our regional rhetorical identity in subtle, yet destructive ways.

Chapter 8 looks at how some educational programs within the region have worked to resist deficit ideology in successful ways. By making rhetoric and identity an important part of students' educational experiences, teachers can make school a more central, less alienating experience for those who may come to the classroom with very different expectations and attitudes. The final chapter encapsulates these issues, asking why it matters whether Appalachian students learn to examine and critique their home rhetorics and identities—their "stories"—or not. It matters specifically because feelings of alienation from the types of writing, rhetoric, and identities presented by the educational system can have serious effects on how our students think about themselves and others, let alone their communities and social prospects. Rhetorical sovereignty, the concept that undergirds so much of my project, requires a willingness and ability to interrogate the aspects of our identities we shape and that are shaped by others in ways we want to embrace or resist. Without this knowledge, the chance to decide for ourselves who we are, as individuals or communities, and how we want to be presented becomes nearly impossible to attain.

When I first encountered the concept of rhetorical sovereignty in Lyons's essay, it felt like a revelation. Lyons argued that cultural groups had the right to make writing fit their own desires and needs.[3] What follows in this book is my attempt to do just that, to understand and write an aspect of my cultural rhetoric in the way that it asks to be written. It is my rhetorical quilt. It's my assembled story of how I've come to understand one aspect of the rhetoric in which I was raised and how it has shaped me as a writer. It's a rhetorical tradition that values individuality; in other words, my experiences, my quilt, may be different from one you'd craft your-self. But that doesn't mean it has less value, or that there's nothing you can take from witnessing it. We tell our stories so that they can be shared, so that those who can find meaning in our experiences can benefit from them. A story, once heard, becomes part of your experience, too.

I'll tell you some of mine.

CHAPTER 1

Ethos

The concept of ethos (the Greek root for the word ethics) in rhetorical study traces back to Aristotle, who argued that trustworthiness was essential in a credible speaker. To be heard and believed, one must be able to prove one's ethical character. In modern academic writing, ethos includes the moves writers make to establish their credibility, including things like citing experts on the topic at hand. Ethos matters to Appalachian rhetoric too, as I've experienced it, but I've noticed that there are particular methods for creating it. It's established by foregrounding roots, family ties, and place-connections. Ethos comes from establishing a voice that doesn't differentiate itself from the audience, that doesn't present its ideas as more provable or logical than what the audience might have; it comes from saying that I am one of you, I am part of this place, of these people.

This is my ethos.

The stories I tell are part of my experience. Maybe they will echo ones you've heard, or maybe they can encourage you to think about your own. That's something I've found the most useful ones do. So, let me tell you a story.

Like most of the stories I think of as mine, this one started before I was born. "Pap" is a regional term meaning grandfather; I grew up knowing that my Pap's own grandparents had built what was known in our family as the old house. I never knew them, of course, nor even Pap's mother, the last person to live in it, but I knew their house intimately. The old house was unlivable by the time I was born, and when I think on it, it's the sagging walls and rotted out floors that I remember. It stood there, thirty feet from the front porch of our trailer, till I was fourteen. As a child, I could sit on our porch in summertime to watch the once-white curtains blowing through a broken window on the old house and imagine I was seeing a ghost. It wasn't scary, really, the old house or the spirits in it. They were family.

And what a family to have. William Gallagher (the first) built the old house with his mother, wife, and kids after he came home from the Civil War. We have a picture of him in his Union uniform, crossing his pistol and knife in front of his chest, defiant and strong. War may have tempered these traits a bit before the end. Having survived the Battle of South Mountain and, barely, Antietam, he never had a good word to say about war when he told his kids about it. In fact, me and Mom had to rediscover the names of his battles because these weren't what got passed down to us. Individual battle names were, in the family memory, forgotten. Instead, what we learned from him, like his children and his children's children, was that war was hell. The story goes that he would tell his children, "I run five miles to get into the army. And once I was in it, I'd a-run ten to git out, and been glad just to go *home*." William's father went into battle at his side, and he never did come back from it. Dying away from home: wasn't much worse you could say about war than that.

I know my ancestors' names and stories and words from what got told generation to generation. Writing didn't tell the stories, mouths did, but sometimes written words featured in the stories themselves. Inside the old house was the letter informing William's mother that her husband, Elza, was dead in some forsaken war hospital in Tennessee and for a price could be brought home for burial. (She couldn't pay. In Tennessee he remained.) I know that my great-great-grandmother, Sarah Narcissus, held together her family and families around her as a root doctor. The old house kept two well-worn volumes of herb lore and advice on home mainte-nance to scaffold the learning she likely got from her own momma, even though their pages had long since become so crumbled and mildewed as to be mostly unreadable. The old house held the albums containing tin-type photos of relations whose names were documented, but about whom we've lost all else. It held the Bibles my great-grandmother Maud Lula's father had used when he was a preacher at the Baptist church on the next hill over. All of these were held on to, not because of what their writings could tell us, but as artifacts around which stories were told, remembrances kept.

Grandma, Pap, and Mom eventually agreed that the old house should come down, as it was getting dangerous for the kids to play around those sagging walls and broken windows. I don't believe any consideration other than our safety would have made that decision possible. Pap called a neighbor, who had a backhoe, to see about doing the job. What we didn't realize was that this neighbor would take to the task with initiative. He showed up the next day while we were all gone at work and school and with his backhoe pushed the old house, including so many of its precious contents, over into the wooded holler below and crushed the remnants into pieces in his tracks. I came home from school to find that those walls, by which I'd measured my life up until then, were gone completely.

But the place remains, and the stories with it, and that is what we hold to. Not long after that my parents, brother, and I moved out of the trailer and into a house we'd had built a little further out the ridge, and my cousin moved into the trailer. Eventually, she would add to the family two babies, and when they'd outgrown the trailer, she had a double-wide moved in to the precise spot where the old house had been. The location of the old house is a place that centers the extent of our farmland, bracketed by my parents' home on one end and my grandparents' on the other. All told, the blood of seven generations of Gallaghers have lived on this land; the houses come and go, yet the land remains, the pole around which we seem to rotate.

Is there something rhetorical in it, then, these generations, these stories, these artifacts, this place? In other words, is it part of how I learned to identify myself and to communicate that identity? Did it communicate to me about what was good and right and worth expressing? The short answer is yes, but it isn't an answer I've always known consciously. Yet these are the most recent incarnations of questions I've considered for years, since the day one of my middle-school English teachers told us we were Appalachian and perhaps even before then. There was never, at least in my family, a time when it was overtly and specifically stated: this here is your home. It's who you are. So where did I get the *sense* of it so strongly? I'd noticed since I first started to make sense of stories that ours weren't much like the ones I saw on TV. I noticed differences in how people talked, lived, and interacted, even before I'd noticed the value judgments people could and did make about these. Questions about the sources of these differences, their causality and implications, have been with me, then, since childhood. In rhetorical studies, I've found what seems to be the most holistic way of gathering and considering these questions that has yet been shown to me. It was through the field's scholars, like Geneva Smitherman, Victor Villanueva, and Shirley Brice Heath, that concepts of culture, rhetoric, and literacy became for me interwoven. Through them, I learned to extrapolate the questions they asked about specific cultural groups' "ways with words" to my situation: does my upbringing affect how I write and think? Do my family stories, and the places and things around which they revolve, connect us with something bigger than just us, some-thing my English teacher perceived in her reference to us as "Appalachian?"

I would posit that there is something deeply rhetorical in the large, messy conglomeration of places, peoples, stories, and more that fills my mind when I try to think and write my identity, but by a definition of the term I'm not sure I've encountered. While rhetoric as an academic field has a distinguished history of theo-rizing and exploring diverse definitions, the version of rhetoric I received in college-prep English classes, in the form of "academic writing," conveyed an idea that students from the classical era onward might have recognized. Rhetoric, by their definition, was about writing arguments. Specifically, it was about writing rig-idly organized and worded arguments intended, at least in theory, to change readers' minds. Often, this persuasion involved defining and defending a preapproved thesis statement, on a pre-approved, academically acceptable topic. The story of the old house had no place in any academic writing assignment I ever received in high school, no matter how deeply it remained in my psyche. School writing was for making and defending arguments about great literature, regardless of how deeply uncertain I felt about the arguments I was making. Undoubtedly I experienced, as many scholars have noticed with many student populations, a fundamental difference in the values of home versus school com-munication. But I have since come to suspect that defining my discomfort as a values-clash overlooks something perhaps even more deeply fundamental. That perhaps it was the conception of writing, and even communication itself, as rooted in thesis state-ments and the persuasion of others that symbolized an even greater rift. Maybe I wasn't just encountering differences in sub-ject matter or grammar. Maybe I had, though I didn't realize it then, different ideas about what communication was for at all.

———

The first time I met Anna, about five years back, we talked about West Virginia. She grew up there, and I had some family history in the state, so we canvassed surnames for any potential common relations or acquaintances. While we didn't talk about geography—the hills or rivers or coal mines—from my perspective our subject was *place*, in that the peoples themselves, and our instinct to discuss them, is part of the place by definition. However, the subject of place in any form didn't come up again until months later (with both of us having just started grad school, school subjects formed by far the bulk of our conversations, with little time for much else). Somehow, we got started discussing our writing weaknesses. I'd just gotten feedback on a paper to the effect that I didn't have a strong thesis, that the overall tone of my argument was too tentative. "That happens to me a lot," I admitted, feeling pretty ashamed of myself for routinely failing such a basic tenet of academic writing, even after all these years of practice. But Anna shrugged it off. "They just don't get that it's because you're Appalachian," she said. "You don't want to tell anyone what to think." Anna described my conundrum perfectly: thesis statements and classical arguments have always *felt wrong*. And on greater reflection, I think it's only the start of how and why my senses of rhetoric, writing, and communication have never entirely meshed, at least not comfortably, with the most common textbook definitions of rhetorical correctness.

I spent several years teaching at a research university within Appalachia. Despite its regional location, the bulk of my students were from outside the area—mostly from suburban northern or central Ohio and mostly with college-preparatory educational backgrounds. They tended to have experience, if not fluency, with the types of writing and literacy they were expected to utilize in school. I remember teaching a junior-level course that incorporated world Englishes and rhetorics; in an early session, I asked my students how they would feel if they had to write in a rhetorical schema different from the academic writing they were used to. One student asked, "You mean, you would want us to write in some made up way?" I find this question deeply significant: the conventions of academic writing were so normalized to her that any other way felt unnatural, made up.

Later, when I taught a composition course entitled "Writing about Environmental Sustainability," the student population was similar: non-Appalachian students who, while they may not have been perfect at utilizing the conventions of academic composition—thesis statements, topic sentences, support, etc.—certainly recognized and attempted them without much forethought. Our opening class writing project was called a place-based biography. In order to get students to think about "the environment" as something immediate, as influential in their lives, I asked them to think and write about how places have shaped them in important ways. Many students chose as a thesis some particular aspect of their personality or a personal value that they held (along the lines of a "This I Believe" statement). They then discussed an interaction they'd had in a specific location that helped them build or demonstrate these values. Others chose to focus more on a place itself, with a thesis stating the dominant impression they wanted their readers to get about the place ("Such and such is a great place to raise a family because . . . ," for example).

However, one student went in a different direction. Marc, the only student in my class who, like me, hailed from Appalachia, lacked a thesis statement of any sort in his essay draft. Rather, his essay told a collection of stories about differing aspects of his homeplace. In our discussions, I pointed out that some readers might find his essay disorganized; they might not understand why a description of a particular tree in his backyard was followed by the story of his community's response to a high school classmate's car accident. Marc had a question for me, then, one I think is important: why did the reader need to know anything beyond the fact that these ideas were connected for *him*, that these were things he thought about when describing his sense of place? For him, this essay didn't need a thesis. It was, rather, a way of demonstrating for a reader his own sense of what living in his community felt like and why. But he also pointed out that living there could mean very different things to others; he was wary of making a definitive statement about his hometown at the expense of other interpretations. He liked his hometown, but should he write a thesis about how good it was, when not everyone was bound to agree? Wouldn't it be better to just think about and share some of his favorite stories and let everyone else decide for themselves whether a place like his was good? Marc's essay was, I've come to think, his quilt, a text that could very well mean more for him in composing it, than for his readers in reading it.

On reflection, I feel like I recognize what Marc was doing because I have done writing projects like it myself, frequently and unintentionally—even those that were intended to be classical arguments. I would have no thesis, or a very weak one. What I would do instead was essentially write my way through my thought process on a particular subject. I would show my readers what experiences or ideas the topic illuminated for me or that influenced how I thought about the subject at hand. For a long time, I didn't necessarily understand that I wasn't trying to make an argument, per se. If asked, I probably would have said that I was because I knew that was what an academic essay was supposed to do. But what I was ultimately doing, rather than pushing for my reader to agree with a particular point, was showing them how I thought, how *I* reached the conclusion that I did about a subject. Likewise,

Marc was uncomfortable with crafting a thesis, the "dominant idea," about his experience because making one thing about his community dominant would by necessity denigrate other things, aspects that might have more meaning for others than for him. A thesis would risk telling others what to think about his community instead, he would just show them how he felt. *He* knew what he thought about his homeplace, and he could tell the stories that made him think that way. His reader could witness his experience, could perhaps agree with him (or not), and could view his process as an example from which to think about their own perspectives on their own homeplaces.

The problem, as I see it, is that an academic reader also might do none of these things, or even realize that doing these things is part of Marc's rhetorical purpose. Even less likely are they to understand why this purpose feels valid to him, when he can't articulate it himself. According to Marc, this was his first experience of considering his rhetorical effects, let alone trying to explain why he made these rhetorical moves. Marc defined himself as Appalachian for much the same reason I initially did: he was told in school that that was what he was. Also, he evinced in his essay many of the social concepts I have come to think of as commonly Appalachian, beyond even his style of writing and essay organization, not only in the stories he told, but also their themes: place, family, faith, and local history all intertwined for Marc. But what he didn't do, at least initially, was connect his way of writing and rhetoric *with* his Appalachian identity. He thought that he was simply fulfilling a writing assignment to the best of his ability, and he felt little hope of actually doing it well. In short, Marc didn't recognize that his rhetorical approach was based on cultural or place influence, which I strongly suspect it was. Instead, he had only a vague sense that his way of writing wasn't "right." And if he couldn't recognize the cultural reasoning behind his rhetoric, how could his writing teachers, many of whom come from entirely different place and cultural backgrounds, be expected to?

What Marc was doing in that paper, and what I've since noticed other Appalachian students doing in other papers, was writing an "argument" in an Appalachian style, without an explicit opening thesis, by demonstrating his own subjective process of thinking through an idea and establishing himself as one with the people and place he wrote about. In doing so, he validated that the topic itself was one worth thinking about—which stories of our experiences in places are most relevant to us as individuals? It wasn't always clear to me, the reader, why he went from one idea or story to the next. He may not even have been able to articulate why if asked. But they were ideas that fit for him. What I began to consider from his essay was that gathering and sharing our stories is a valid way of sharing ideas, a way that comes from a people, a place, and a history. I have come to believe that greater visibility for this understanding can benefit these students, this region, and the academic realms with which we are making ever more contact.

———

It is the melding of my personal and textual encounters and experiences, some quite old, some quite recent, and some encountered by me only vicariously through other people's stories, that has prompted my interest in what I think of as Appalachian rhetoric, or at least, as *my* Appalachian rhetoric. I make this distinction in recognition that Appalachia is vast, is complex, and means different things to different people. And the factors influencing these interpretations are multiple, not limited only to subsets of regional geography. My experience of Appalachia has been that of a rural farming culture and economy; this is not the Appalachia experienced by everyone. Todd Snyder's *The Rhetoric of Appalachian Identity* explores the possibilities offered by critical pedagogy in

Appalachian classrooms. Yet the Appalachia he describes is not entirely identical with mine. He grew up in a coal town, where mining was not only the primary economic activity, it also dominated people's lives and educations. Even political thought and action were dictated by the coal industry. In his experience, Appalachian identity is at least in part something dictated to people by corporations, with self-serving intent. For me, the pathway to Appalachian identity has been different. Yet, neither of these identities is less valid.

I cannot possibly, then, provide a definition of Appalachianness that will satisfy everyone, if such a definition even exists (which I doubt). Some might feel that by not fixing specific traits to Appalachian identity, I am in fact generalizing that identity based on my own. That is far from my intent. What I am doing is saying that just because my Appalachian identity is mine, not everyone's, doesn't mean it has no value. The act of making this distinction—of attempting to validate my own experience and reading of rhetorical constructions without denigrating those of others—to my mind fits deeply with the Appalachian rhetorical stylings I've encountered in my experience and research. It is a rhetoric, I submit, that allows for both individual interpretation and humility in the face of alternatives, that can accept ambiguity and multiplicity. It is a rhetoric that seeks connection over argumentation, or at least, over what many would recognize as academic argumentation. But I'm perhaps getting ahead of the story. What I posit here is simply that there is an inner life to the Appalachian rhetoric I've encountered that can engender in its people cultural and communicative values that have traditionally been little explored. What I seek to explore further is the shape of my own regional Appalachian rhetoric, to see what influences it and how it influences identity, and perhaps most importantly, to show why these differences can matter, within and outside the geographic region.

What does it matter if anyone understands Appalachia or Appalachian rhetoric? I think it matters for us, specifically for the reasons Lyons's describes in his article: our identities and how we feel about them can have everything to do with our sense of self-worth, self-determination, whether or not we learn to "decolonize the mind."[1] And it matters for how others treat us and our differences.

There is a story that I think of, in broad terms, as my exigency. It's another one that starts before I was born. In fact, I could say it starts with the successive generations of my family that have been raised on our homeplace for the past 150 years. My mother and her sisters, daughters of William (the second) and Alberta Gallagher, have remained here in eastern Ohio, near both the western border of Pennsylvania and the northern border of West Virginia. All my cousins on that side of the family grew up practically within shouting distance of the original Gallagher land, while my brother and I were raised on it. One of my cousins, upon reaching adulthood, has returned to this land permanently. The current geography of the homeplace is something like this: take a dirt road up a hill until you reach my grandparents' house; my cousin and her two children are in a double-wide a little ways further up the hill from that, and my parents' house is a little further out the ridge from that. We are the only family on this hilltop, our houses connected by that dirt road, all within easy walking distance of each other. It is a situation not at all uncommon in our region.

When I was fourteen, we moved out of our trailer and into the aforementioned house my parents built, while my cousin Sadie moved into the trailer. By this point, Sadie had completed her degree and had met Ron. Ron was from further north, where he was used to flatter land, a suburban lifestyle, and an idea of "family" that was, we would come to learn, much narrower than ours. When they married, the plan was that they would settle here on the homeplace.

After the wedding and the birth of their first child, this decision began to unravel. It became clear that Ron didn't expect that, when he married Sadie, he married her family. Once, when Sadie cut her hand and needed stitches, she called her mother to drive her to the emergency room—I would have done the same. It's even a joke with us—if you're sick or hurt, you call your mom. If you can't find her, call your grandma. Ron was angry, however, that she hadn't called him at work, instead. It was another example of how Sadie was, he said more than once, "too attached to her family." Nor did he seem pleased by the fact that weekends meant days spent with grandparents, aunts, uncles, and cousins. Ron, having chosen not to sell his house in a northern suburb, soon began insisting Sadie and their baby travel there with him on weekends. However, even during the week, he'd start up arguments that ended with threats of divorce if Sadie didn't agree to make a more permanent change. At one point, Ron took their son to his home without telling her and refused to return him unless she agreed to move. He relented, however, and this pattern of volatile behavior continued throughout her pregnancy with their second child. Divorce came quickly after, along with his remarriage to someone who more closely shared his regional/cultural background.

I don't wish to indicate that any distinct breach inevitably exists between the lifestyles and values of people who come from different backgrounds, or those who live in urban settings versus those that live in rural ones, either inside or outside of Appalachia (and yes, there is such a thing as urban Appalachia). Any moves that attempt to concretize differences are often made in the service of racist or culturally chauvinist ideologies. What I find intriguing in this case, however, is just how surprising Ron seemed to find it that these kinds of differences existed at all. I'm sure many people like Ron, who were used to a single lifestyle surrounded by urban conveniences, would be disoriented by a rural lifestyle surrounded by family members who are all well-versed in the day-to-day minutia of one's life . . . a style of living we perceived as normal. Each of them, ultimately, wanted to live in incompatible ways. If the story had ended there, I likely wouldn't be telling it now. However, the story didn't end, and place, culture, and lifestyle became even more central to it.

Though initially granted weekend visitation, Ron and his new wife eventually sought full custody of the children. We all knew that what the kids heard on their visits up at their father's house was not flattering or even respectful toward their mother or her family. Ron told them at length how much more fun life at his home would be because there would be "so much more to do" in town than there was back in the country. But the distinctions he tried to make went beyond a preference for urban or rural living; they crossed into issues of culture—what families were, as well as what they were supposed to do, have, and instill. He chided his son for being close to his mother and her family; this made him a "mamma's boy," who had too many family members ready to "wipe his butt for him" when things got difficult in his life. Ron's new wife claimed that the children lacked "essential" mannerisms, such as being able to hold their eating utensils "properly," something ascribed to their being raised by "hillbillies." And when Ron and his new wife bought clothes and toys for the children, they were told that none of these could be brought home, as "nice" things would not be appropriate in their mother's house. Ultimately, what was being made here was, in my mind, a very disturbing distinction: the difference between Ron's lifestyle and ours was, according to him, not one of culture and preference, but one of a right way to live and think, versus a wrong one.

It's a point that came to a head in the charges Ron made to the courts as part of his custody case. Ron could show that with their mother, the children lived with a single parent who, technically, was below the poverty line. Specifically, he argued that he and his new wife could provide the children a "stable family environment," where the primary family members (i.e., a father and a mother) lived under one roof and where presumably grandparents would be seen only on holidays and cousins perhaps at annual family reunions, rather than daily. The normal boundaries of American nuclear family life would be established and maintained. Likewise, their (suburban) location was more conducive to the children's well-being and social development than their current (rural) environment. The environment of their mother's home lacked the mainstream American normality they would receive nearer Cleveland. In other words, the court was being asked in this case to remove the children from an impoverished, single, backwoods-dwelling mother and grant them to a middle-class, urban, nuclear family unit.

The case did not ultimately go to trial; Ron withdrew his custody suit the day before trial was scheduled to begin, for reasons we will probably never know—though we suspect this was evidence his new marriage was not as solid as he had hoped it would appear to a judge. But what continues to worry me is that on paper, and to a court, Ron's assertions may well have had merit. However, what they left out, and they left out a lot, has everything to do with a convenient (and from my point of view, deeply unfortunate) failure to view Appalachia on its own terms. Patricia Williams puts forward the race- and culture-blind rhetoric of the United States legal system as a tragic flaw. The law's presumed objective neutrality in fact reflects the biases of those empowered to make legal decisions:

> Law and legal writing aspire to formalized, color-blind, liberal ideals. Neutrality is the standard for assuring these ideals; yet the adherence to it is often determined by reference to an aesthetic of uniformity, in which difference is simply omitted . . . Race-neutrality in law has become the presumed antidote for race bias in real life.[2]

Because the law presumes itself above such distinctions, Appalachia has little place in a courtroom; little consideration is given to the convenience with which "objective" legal values and the social values of mainstream, white American culture coincide.

Because Appalachian cultural values are rendered invisible in the American legal system, my voice in the case, as the children's mother's cousin, amounted to nothing. How could anyone who didn't live the way we did be expected to understand that a parent's cousin could be a daily part of her children's lives and the children a part of hers? That losing them would create the kind of wound that would never heal not only for their mother, but also for multiple generations of extended family? Or even, come to that, that a woman would be more willing to risk divorce than to raise her children anywhere but a rural hillside farm? The answer to these questions would require an understanding of the web of our lives, a web built by peoples, by places, and by words that go unheard far too often by those outside our region. In fact, Ron's arguments played very nicely on the "common sense" of mainstream America: he offered a nuclear, financially well-off family situation in a suburban environment, whereas their mother offered a double-wide in the woods, at least a half-hour's drive from a more or less urban setting, and the salary of a substitute school teacher. How could the kids possibly be considered better off here?

I understand how. But it's not an understanding I've ever been called on to put into words, particularly written words. How can all of this, these ways of living and dying, of thinking and speaking and simply *being* in the world, be adequately explained to those who haven't lived them since birth? How can we explain who we are when I don't think many of us have conceptualized it for ourselves? And how can we make ourselves heard by those who don't want to listen? Maybe, for a start, we just don't stop talking.

I find that education, specifically in terms of rhetoric, plays significantly into this case. When what we've been taught to value, and how we've been taught it, is not surfaced or discussed, encounters with difference can more easily slip into binaries: us, them. Right, wrong. Nowhere in the court documents was cultural difference raised as a factor in this case, although its effects (including the rhetorical construction of "family" and the comparative values for place, money, and history) certainly were. But why not? Ron's construction of my family as impoverished and backward, even unstable, is not necessarily viewed as a culturally influenced, rhetorically instilled bias; in the discourse of mainstream social values, it is simple truth. Such mainstream discourse holds that to have a low income is to be poor, which is to be ignorant, which is to be *wrong*; to knowingly choose to live in a region of fewer economic opportunities exemplifies this ignorance and backwardness. To want this for your children is tantamount to abuse. And when this discourse prevails in the realms of power, the realms that will decide on an Appalachian child's best interest, not knowing how to hear alternate discourses becomes anything but fair and objective.

But what if alternate constructions were allowed? What if the truths constructed about us could be augmented by those we provide? What would they even sound like? Of course these questions themselves are based on an assumption I'm making, that I feel justified in making, which says that the home-life of Sadie and her kids is an enactment of cultural difference, one with its own values and means of communicating those values. My assumption rests, ultimately, on the idea that such things as Appalachian cultures and rhetorics exist and that the ways we embody and enact them can, and should, be more widely understood.

The first question many might reasonably ask is, if Appalachian cultures and rhetorics exist and shape identity, then what exactly are they? What is Appalachian identity? While I stand by my point that no one definition of Appalachian identity exists, I can say that there is a fairly simple geographic answer to the question of what

Appalachia is. The Appalachian Regional Commission (ARC), established by Congress in 1965, defines Appalachia thusly:

> The Appalachian Region . . . is a 205,000-square-mile region that follows the spine of the Appalachian Mountains from southern New York to northern Mississippi. It includes all of West Virginia and parts of 12 other states: Alabama, Georgia, Kentucky, Maryland, Mississippi, New York, North Carolina, Ohio, Pennsylvania, South Carolina, Tennessee, and Virginia.[3]

It's a flat, technical definition, as it is no doubt intended to be. Appalachians are people living in the Appalachian region. However, a truer definition is far more complicated because it needs to account for the many Appalachian peoples who no longer live in the region. Is Appalachian identity something that magically stops the minute a person's feet hit flat land? Of course not, because geography is only half the story of something that encapsulates far greater complexities. The only sense we get about life experience in the ARC definition comes later:

> The Appalachian Region's economy, once highly dependent on mining, forestry, agriculture, chemical industries, and heavy industry, has become more diversified in recent times, and now includes manufacturing and professional service industries. In 1965, one in three Appalachians lived in poverty. Over the 2007–2011 period, the Region's poverty rate was 16.1 percent. The number of Appalachian counties considered economically distressed was 223 in 1965; in fiscal year 2014 that number is 93.[4]

Again, we are defined (through an ostensibly objective standard) by poverty, albeit a poverty less severe than before, thanks to the efforts of the Appalachian Regional Commission, who define their own mission in four points:

1) Increase job opportunities and per capita income in Appalachia to reach parity with the nation.
2) Strengthen the capacity of the people of Appalachia to compete in the global economy.
3) Develop and improve Appalachia's infrastructure to make the Region economically competitive.
4) Build the Appalachian Development Highway System to reduce Appalachia's isolation.[5]

I have no wish to denigrate the ARC's work, especially now that federal budget cuts have potentially put the entire organization on the chopping block. However, I do think it's worth noting that if one were to encounter Appalachia solely by the information provided through the ARC, it would be easy to assume that Appalachia has no culture to explore or to celebrate, or even to denigrate; at least none different than any other part of the United States. It is this silence on the idea of Appalachian cultures, as much as any denigration of those cultures, that I find unsettling.

But why? Why does it matter how Appalachia is defined, or whether its rhetoric is perceived and appreciated? It matters, I think, because these perceptions can affect our sense of identity, and by extension, how we exist and how we allow ourselves to be defined. J.D. Vance, author of the controversial book *Hillbilly Elegy*, describes an upbringing that is very different from my own, but he also presents a point I find intriguing: that Appalachian people find multiculturalism threatening.[6] An article in the *Atlantic* likewise argues that the fear of multiculturalism, not economics, drove white, working-class voters like those in Appalachia toward supporting Trump in the 2016 election.[7] While it is dangerous to conflate the white working class with Appalachia—because, it bears repeating, not all Appalachians are white working class, nor are all the white working class Appalachian—I think it's a question worth pondering. Is there any truth to this idea, that we are a region definable by our fear of others? If there is, I think the greater question is the following: why don't we see ourselves as *part* of multiculturalism?

Because, at root, I think we should; we should see Appalachia as bringing a cloth to our country's multicultural quilt. I consider myself to be Appalachian. And when I say this, I mean more than that I live in the region of the Appalachian Mountains, a place with a higher poverty rate than many other regions in the United States. I mean that I perceive myself as having developed within a cultural system, one revolving around distinctive rhetorical traditions, based in both region and history. This is not a realization I learned in school; it is one I have determined for myself via study, interaction, and experiences with peoples whose own cultural backgrounds are not Appalachian. I learned to recognize the systems in which I grew and developed at home as being rooted in a non-mainstream rhetoric. And it is only through this study and experience that I have developed interest in the dynamics of Appalachian rhetoric and its treatment.

I mention this because I find it troubling that my development of a conscious sense of cultural self-definition has had to feel so very individual. When I was in school, we didn't discuss cultural values or rhetorics, let alone what creates them or how they shape us. Yet the misunderstandings of what can happen when Appalachian students put pen to paper are still with us. For my part, I've discovered that it isn't accidental that I often think my way through ideas in terms of stories, my own and other peoples'. It isn't accidental that other peoples' stories, particularly peoples from these hills, can come to feel like my own. What I'm starting to see, and what I want to share, is that there is a reason for this that extends beyond me as an individual and into my participation and upbringing in a particularly misconstrued region.

———

Scott Richard Lyons, in his article "Rhetorical Sovereignty: What Do American Indians Want from Writing?," defines the concept of rhetorical sovereignty as a people's control over their own meaning; in other words, it is "the inherent right and ability of peoples to determine their own communicative needs and desires . . . to decide for themselves the goals, modes, styles, and languages of public discourse."[8] This definition is a lens through which to see how writing, education, and identity politics intertwine for marginalized peoples. By Lyons's definition, rhetorical sovereignty requires self-recognition and the recognition by others of cultural identity on the people's terms; therefore, an Appalachian rhetorical sovereignty, if one is possible, would require us to name ourselves and our experiences and for others to respect that naming.

I recognize that my use of Lyons's definition is complicated by the inherent differences in the situations and peoples under discussion. Native American peoples experience political domination, wherein once fully independent nations are now subject to the domination of an outside entity, which is not the case for Appalachia as a people/culture. We are implicated in that domination; it cannot, and should not, be forgotten that my ability to discuss Appalachian regions and peoples is predicated upon the attempted annihilation of the Native peoples from whom the mountains were taken. I don't wish for my exploration of rhetorical sovereignty to be just one more thing my people have taken from his. Lyons's concept of rhetorical sovereignty is dependent on a group's recognition of itself as a people, defined by him as "a group of human beings united together by history, language, culture, or some combination therein—a community joined in union for a common purpose: the survival and flourishing of the people itself."[9] Appalachians are difficult to describe as a "people," not, I think, because we *lack* these connections, but because not enough of us have had the opportunities to recognize them. In other words, too few southeastern Ohioans perceive any links of history, language, and culture joining them to North Carolinians, or Tennesseans to Western Pennsylvanians. Too few of us ever have the chance or a good reason to think about and explore these ties.

Therefore, what I am making here is a very soft connection, in that both the Native peoples Lyons considers and the Appalachian peoples on whom I focus lack rhetorical sovereignty in fundamental ways. Composition and rhetorical studies can play a role in bringing both of us closer to its attainment. (Though the difficulties implicit in Native peoples achieving rhetorical sovereignty are, unfortunately, even greater.) How could deeper explorations of Appalachian rhetoric contribute to a greater sense of our peoplehood, of self-definition? Is it worth seeking? I believe that it is, specifically because I want us all to have access to the forms of self-determination and empowerment Lyons describes. I want us to become more skilled in recognizing what shapes our own identities and in criticizing the ways industrial and political forces prey on them.

I want, too, a greater understanding of why Appalachia has so often played the role of America's educational and social scapegoat. Too often we are defined not as culturally or rhetorically unique but as same-but-worse, as the negative image of American whiteness. We are presented as the same as the American mainstream (white, Anglo-Saxon, Protestant) but undeniably worse due to our own individual freakishness of character (choosing, in essence, to live in poverty, ignorance, and violence). We become the other by which the mainstream defines and contents itself with its own superiority. *We started the same, but we've chosen to be better*, they seem to say. *When we look at Appalachia, we can see how far we've come.*

This is a definition disturbing for its mistaken impression of Appalachia as essentially white, a definition that rhetorically erases the Peoples of Color who have always lived in Appalachia, including its original Native peoples. Yet even within the characterization of Appalachian peoples as essentially white, Victor Villanueva has argued that we become racialized, but as a color without a name.[10] Appalachia is framed as white but not white, as American but not American, in ways that are meant to be readily accepted but not overly critiqued. Because if critiqued, this social construction might well fall apart at the seams.

A wider American disdain for Appalachia has been bred in this silence, this absence of alternate definition. If anything, it's a perception that has proven as useful for the discourse of the powerful as it has destructive for us. Our invisibility has been useful for creating and maintaining the conditions under which the region can be abused. Corporations and extractive industries feel empowered to exploit us economically, while entertainment media find in us ready-made villains for their horror movies and jokes for their comedies. And often educators work to "fix" the flaws in our characters and values that keep us in such sad mental and physical conditions, faithful in the power of standardized discourse to lead us from the darkness.

If Lyons is right, then understanding our rhetorics, how they work and how they influence us, is essential to understanding ourselves and claiming power over what we value, as well as to being seen by others on our own terms. What I've discovered through textual and primary research is that, far from lacking a rhetorical tradition, Appalachian rhetorics can have roots deeper in different regional histories than those influencing academic discourse. In my upcoming chapters, I will explore how Appalachia's rhetorical and cultural history links us to Europe's Celtic fringes (Ireland,

Scotland, and Wales), regions where classical Greco-Roman influence was limited. I have discovered that, at least in my corner of the Appalachians, we have inherited and continue to propagate a rhetoric well-suited for rural regions, one that seeks to create connections rather than distinctions. Therefore, judging this rhetoric through the lens of the Greco-Roman tradition does us a disservice and contributes to our silencing. I want us to see how we can reclaim our own tradition, examine and understand it, more than we have been allowed to do in the past, and to see how writing can help us do this.

I have a deeply emotional stake in wishing for a greater sense of rhetorical sovereignty for Appalachia. Though Lyons does not directly reference the Indian Child Welfare Act, I find his article to be inextricably haunted by it. Originally passed in 1978, this legislation reacted to a long history of assimilation being achieved by the removal of children from their cultures, to be raised instead by white American families. The act at least attempted to acknowledge that robbing these children of their cultural heritage did them, and their cultures, a great injustice. The act questioned the long-held assumption that becoming culturally American was in these children's best interest by providing them with a "better," more civilized lifestyle than their original backgrounds would provide. For centuries, Native peoples have struggled to be heard against a dominant discourse unwilling to critique its own cultural ideology. That the Indian Child Welfare Act exists at all, imperfect as it is, indicates to me that at least some in our country believe that cultural identity matters. Why, then, is it so hard to understand that growing up Appalachian might matter for our children?

Because culture matters to me, and because being Appalachian matters to me, I want us to build a society, an educational system, and a justice system that will not ignore or denigrate our Appalachian cultural identities. But until we can both name ourselves as Appalachians and define for ourselves what that means, what do we have? For one thing, we have a custody battle in which being Appalachian can work against us, but in a way that is not acknowledged and therefore, not assailable. And I fear such will continue to be the case until we can, as Lyons so powerfully argues, learn to write and claim our own rhetorical and cultural identities.

Could there, one day, be an Appalachian Child Protection Act that demands court systems consider the removal of Appalachian children as damaging to them and to their culture? Maybe. But for such a thing to even be conceivable would require recognition, inside and outside Appalachia, of the existence and validity of Appalachian cultures that we seem nowhere near achieving. I am putting forward here that making Appalachian rhetoric more visible academically, particularly in composition studies, can be an important first step, with potential individual, legal, and economic repercussions.

Lyons acknowledges that, in the face of the kinds of cultural and linguistic extinctions resulting when marginalized groups are denied respect and sovereignty, academic composition and rhetoric "can only do so much."[11] It is, however, worth doing; as Lyons quotes Hawaiian nationalist Haunani-Kay Trask: "Thinking in one's own cultural referents leads to conceptualizing in one's own world view which, in turn, leads to disagreement with and eventual opposition to the dominant ideology."[12] Can these ideals be applicable to Appalachia? Do we have cultural referents to think through, world views to conceptualize, non-dominant ideologies with which to challenge the discourses of power? If the answers to these questions are yes, and I think they are, then we have as much to gain by doing (or lose by neglecting) this type of intellectual work as other marginalized groups.

I worry about children like Marc who get the message in school that they don't know how to write correctly and simply go on believing they can't, but I worry also about the ones who internalize these corrections. My concern is not because they have learned the dominant discourse (I am by no means against learning the discourse of power), but because they have assimilated to it, without perhaps ever understanding what it is that has happened or what they have given up. What if my own teacher had never mentioned Appalachia, even in a negative light; who would I think I am today? If I had never been interested or curious enough to seek out alternate ideas about being this mysterious thing, Appalachian, how would I identify myself? Would I think of myself, of my background, as different from the American mainstream, or would I think of it as *less*? Would I correct the people around me when they said "ain't," cringe at my grandfather playing banjo, and despair at having grown up in a place people think of as backward? Would I have gotten to hold my cousin's babies on the days they were born? Would I have thrown my great-grandmother's quilts away because their colors clash?

There are certainly classrooms in which discussions of Appalachian rhetoric and identity happen, as I will explore in a later chapter. What I want is for these to be the rule, not the exception. If not, if Appalachia's distinctive rhetorical/cultural traditions are not brought forward for consideration, and if the region continues to be uncritically defined from the outside predominantly by stereotypical traits such as poverty, if we continue to overlook or even deny our own identities, then stereotypes will continue to take the place of critical consideration, and "Appalachia" will continue to be excluded from discussions, like Ron and Sadie's custody battle, wherein cultural difference could shed valuable light.

It's time for us to learn how to quilt, or to re-learn if we have forgotten. And it's time to hang our quilts for the rest of you'uns to see.

Chapter 2

Language

"Books grow. This one is the outgrowth of my enchanted childhood in a unique area of the state of Ohio, an area that has long been called the Raven Rocks, since large flocks of ravens were known to have gathered here."

—Elsa Crooks Harper, from
An Enchanted Childhood at Raven Rocks

Not too long back, I took a class on rhetorical theory. My final paper was largely concerned with issues of ecology and theory; like with most of the things I write, I somehow meandered around to discussing things from a local perspective. At one point I wrote, "There is little hope that Appalachia will achieve environmental sustainability until the peoples and cultures of the region are seen and respected." I received nearly identical feedback from both a peer reviewer and my instructor that, I'll admit, I found a little bit baffling: *What do you mean?* they asked, *how is one connected to the other?* And I'll also admit I never did get around to addressing this feedback in the essay because I simply didn't know how. *How could they* not *be connected?* Truth be told, I don't feel much better able to explain what I mean now. What I do think is that Harper sees the connection, too. And maybe there's more of us that feel it than can explain it: the idea that the way we think and act and communicate and flat-out *be* in the world connects in some way to place. And when that way of thinking and being feels healthy and respected, it gives that health and respect back to the land from which it grows. Writing Appalachia is, for me, by its nature an act of environmental advocacy.

But as much as that, it's also a work of history. Because for me, these things cannot be separated: people, land, history, culture, and all developed and expressed through rhetoric. (This is a long-winded way of coming around to discussing rhetorical history, I know, but I feel like I spring from a long-winded people.) Ecological writing theory posits that writing and rhetoric operate within a system, wherein "the participants create in part the environment that, in turn, creates the participants."[1] In other words, texts are interconnected with the rhetorical "ecosystems" that create them and that are, through their influence, created by them. My question, for a long time, has been: how did our rhetorical ecosystem come about? What grew it, essentially? If my words and Harper's grow from a particular place, what can we say about the soil there?

A full examination of Appalachia's rhetorical soil would require a detailed history of all the many peoples and cultures shaping the region, and, as it is a very large region, each new holler can have different nuances than the one that came before. Therefore, my exploration will focus on a specific thread of my northern Appalachian region (roughly speaking, western Pennsylvania, northern West Virginia, and eastern Ohio). Focusing on this region's rhetorical ecosystem is not to say that it differs substantially from other parts of Appalachia, or that it isn't made up of many more complexities than I am able to trace in any one book. What I'm doing is simply starting with one thread and seeing where it takes me.

I want to start my exploration of the cultural history of Appalachian rhetoric with language, specifically because language is the aspect of Appalachian communication that most often takes the spotlight. Whole books can be, and have been, written on the varieties of terms and pronunciations appearing in Appalachian dialects. Language differences can be distinct across, or within, different cultural groups, and this region is no exception. But language is only one feature of literacy, rhetoric, even identity—it alone isn't the whole story. To overstate the importance of dialect risks minimizing the presence of Appalachian cultural and rhetorical influences for anyone whose home discourse doesn't sound the way it "ought" to. If my accent differs from that of someone in Tennessee or in Kentucky, does that by definition make my sense of Appalachian identity less valid?

However, neither should language be something underestimated in its power to influence a sense of identity and expression. I had a student once who wrote an essay on why she wasn't "a hillbilly." Penultimate among the reasons she, despite living in the region all her life, was not really "one of them" had to do with language: she knew "how to talk right." Somewhere along the line, this student had absorbed several things: 1) being Appalachian (a "hillbilly") was a bad thing, 2) membership in this group came down ultimately to language use, and 3) she spoke the "right" way, meaning she need not fear being seen as part of this group.

I, on the other hand, have never seen my Appalachian identity as something to disavow. Rather, I have struggled to maintain my home language in academic contexts where it isn't typically found, a struggle that makes recalling my dialect particularly challenging at those times when I do need it. When I open my mouth to speak at conferences about Appalachian rhetoric, I find myself wondering: *am I what they expected? Do I sound "authentic" enough? How would I talk if I were at home right now? Would I use more double-negatives? Should I use them now?* And, let's be honest, language use is *gonna* be different across such a wide regional expanse, not to mention accounting for varying degrees of experience or assimilation one encounters with other dialects. Ultimately, my concern is that if we focus on language too much, we (as teachers or as students) may miss other significant cultural influences on the texts

Appalachian writers produce. When we miss these influences, it's far easier to disregard a missing thesis statement as a mistake, or a rambling story about a students' grandmother as a lack of organizational awareness.

———

However, because language is so prominent in how audiences encounter and interpret multicultural texts, I would like to consider in more depth how history can affect Appalachian language and why these influences might be important to consider. My own interest in cultural influences on language stems from research into African American Vernacular English (AAVE). My awareness of this field and the debates surrounding language politics has been a slow, sometimes painful development. I was probably around fifteen when what was then called the Oakland Ebonics debate hit the US news cycle in a big way. And I'll be honest: it confused the hell out of me. My limited understanding of the issue was that schools in California were proposing to teach students with accents *in* accents ("accent" being the only term I had for anything like a concept of dialect—neither accent nor dialect being directly discussed in my middle- or high-school classes). Meaning, I thought, that they were simply going to stop teaching students to talk right. I could not at all understand this. Why wouldn't anyone want to learn how to talk right?

Because dialect, let alone an idea of culturally based rhetoric, was absent from any part of my earliest academic experience, I had little idea how to frame concepts of language beyond "right" (meaning Standard English) and "wrong"—meaning everything else. And that "wrong" most definitely included aspects of how I talked at home and how my parents and grandparents talked in unguarded moments. (I say "unguarded" because, like many mothers, mine felt compelled to correct my speech at times; "Say '*she* and *I,*' not '*me* and *her.*'") These were concepts ripe for confusion. I felt shame toward myself when I spoke wrong; "'ain't' isn't a word,"[2] and all that. Of course, plenty of my classmates couldn't a-gave a damn one way nor the other, a disinterest in "correctness" that has probably helped our dialect survive. But I wanted to be a good student, and that meant not questioning the worksheets telling us that *they was* was somehow less logical than *they were*. Even now I can't quite square how I was so easily shamed by my "wrong" English. I'd have been furious if anyone had accused my grandparents, for example, of stupidity on the basis of their English, but I easily believed it of myself and was willing, at least for a time, to believe it of other non-standard speakers. Corrections to my writing, as when I failed to produce and defend strong thesis statements, shamed me too, but I was even less able to see these as anything other than my own personal failings, certainly not as anything cultural. Whereas my family and community taught me my "wrong" speech, and thus gave me a reason to be at least ambivalently protective of it, school alone taught me to write. And when they said I did it badly, well, what alternative did I have but to believe that was true?

It wasn't until college, and the discovery of scholars like Geneva Smitherman, that my worldview opened in a substantive way. Oddly enough, I can't recall the specific context in which I first encountered Smitherman's work, whether it was for a class, a project, or simply my own curiosity. I just recall being suddenly startled into a greater understanding of the possible meanings behind non-standard Englishes through her passionate and undeniably logical 1999 exploration of Ebonics (now more commonly referred to as AAVE):

> Ebonics is emphatically not "broken" English, nor "sloppy" speech. Nor is it merely "slang." Nor is it some bizarre form of language spoken by baggy-pants-wearing Black youth.

Ebonics is a set of communication patterns and practices resulting from Africans' appropriation and transformation of a foreign tongue during the African Holocaust.[3]

The idea that language, and even the patterns and ideas underpinning language use, could indicate not misunderstandings of correct English but rather the influence of a cultural heritage was certainly not one I had encountered on any grammar worksheets. By connecting language not only to current culture, but also to cultural history, Smitherman opened a door for me to consider my own language, and the languages of those around me, in a new way. But what are the chances that every Appalachian kid will eventually read Geneva Smitherman? If I could count on that happening, I could count on this being a better world than it is.

———

I spent several years as an adjunct instructor and tutor at a community college in Appalachia. I'd earned my master's degree and did what many of us hill kids want to do after college and can't: I went home. Of course, this was only possible for me because I had no children to support, could live at home rent-free, was healthy enough to white-knuckle my way through a few years without health insurance, and could just about make do on any other expenses with an adjunct's salary. I could, more or less, afford to choose staying in my homeland. Some of my dearest friends had been forced to move to Columbus or other places in order to make a living. So having this choice made me, among my peers, quite privileged.

And my community college students by and large felt the same about wanting to stay home. They were going to school so they could get the jobs that would support their families and would, specifically, support them *here*. Business majors wanted to open businesses here, nursing majors wanted to work with patients here, electricians wanted to wire homes here. On the other hand, I later got the sense with my university students that, for many of them, school was a means of *escaping* home. For my community college students, school and its attendant costs was the price one paid to afford staying at home. Staying home has become, in Appalachia, something of a pay-to-play enterprise.

I have reason to believe, though, that the community college itself was less enthusiastic about "home," at least in terms of what being at home in Appalachia entailed, than its students were. It was while I was tutoring that the school invited a representative from educational consultant Ruby Payne's Aha! Program to speak with faculty about the economic issues facing our students. I didn't make it to the speech, but I deeply regretted later that I hadn't. Because, apparently, the focus of the session came around heavily to language—specifically, the role non-standard dialect usage played in maintaining our students' "generational poverty" mind-sets[4]: ways of thinking, essentially, that kept most of them from truly progressing into what the teachers thought of as the middle class. Within weeks after the session, the newly inspired English and Communications departments united to form the "Banned Terms Project."

An email was sent to all faculty and instructors to let us know that the school would focus on one "banned term" per month. As we were told, "You might announce the banned term and then in conversations with students or perusal of their written work, you can concentrate on eradicating the phrase in any way you choose."[5] The first banned term was "I seen," while for the second month we would focus on eradicating "we/they was."

The Banned Terms Project seemed to be doing something more than trying to teach students standard English, the language of power; in fact, it seemed poised to enthrone it as the *only* acceptable language.[6] What it didn't do was give any indication of seeing the terms being banned as part of a dialect, part of a culture, which might mean something for us. Given my aforementioned encounters with scholars like Smitherman, I was deeply unsettled with this particular approach. Or, I could say, *I seen* it differently than my colleagues did. If Smitherman's AAVE speakers were demonstrating heritage through their language, their cultural diversity, then could the same not be said for Appalachian students? Could making it known that the college planned, overtly and proudly, to standardize students' dialects send the very oppressive messages that Smitherman cautions us against?

When I was working with a student from a developmental writing course, I had something of a crisis of conscience. One-on-one tutoring was still relatively new to me and I was learning how to work with students across a wide spectrum of needs, so I was still unsure of myself, even without the added pressure of banning terms. I didn't quite know how to broach the subject when I noticed one of the banned terms in her sentence.

"Umm . . . ok. See this part right here?" She looked at the words I'd circled: *I seen.* "Oh," she said. "Is that one of them banned words?"

"Yeah," I said, embarrassed to be saying so. After all, I used "I seen" myself.

"Okay." She picked up her own pen and put a mark beside the term. I was about to ask her what she thought to replace it with, when she added, "It feels wrong, you know?"

I was pretty sure I did. But I asked, "What do you mean?"

"Well, my teacher says that the right way of saying something like this will sound more right when we say it to ourselves. But it don't! This," underlining her term, "is what sounds right. That's how my grandma says it. What's wrong with it?"

Now how was I supposed to answer that?

I sent an email that weekend to the full-time English faculty, four individuals who had been exceptionally kind to me in their assurances that, though an adjunct, I was part of the team and should come to them with any questions or concerns I ever encountered in the classroom. I asked if we could talk about this "Banned Terms Project," specifically about how, in this form, it could have an un-intentioned effect on students' self- and community-esteem. I told them about the student in my tutoring session. I referenced Geneva Smitherman and Keith Gilyard's work on dialect's cultural repercussions, as well as Peter Elbow's calls to "invite the mother tongue" into our classrooms along with the standard. (I thought Gilyard's point that "the eradication of one tongue is not prerequisite to the learning of a second"[7] was particularly relevant in this instance.) Given what I knew about my audience—these were four deeply dedicated and caring teachers—and cognizant of my own inexperience by comparison, I didn't demand a cease and desist. I didn't say that I was personally upset about what was, in its rawest form, a forthright argument that my own mother tongue had no place in academia. I was *diplomatic*.

I received one response. Jennifer, like the other full-time instructors, hailed from outside the region. When we met in the hall the following week, she raised the subject of my email and said, "It basically comes down to this: would you rather our students stayed poor?" She held her hands open in front of her, like she was at a loss for alternative options.

I quit soon after that term.

In trying, as I have many times since, to make sense of this episode to myself, I find that I'm troubled by several things. One, of course, is the idea that non-standard dialects can and should be "eradicated," at least in the realms of academia. That the "right" way to say something will "sound right," if one well and truly "thinks" about it. Another is the easy and uncritical correlation of dialect, and by extension culture, with economic status. Our students were not poor because of any systemic social inequality that makes it difficult to access educational opportunities and jobs that pay fair wages without causing environmental harm or requiring outward migration. No, they were poor because they had never learned the right way to talk. And if one doesn't speak correctly, how can one think correctly? Who would hire such a person? Ultimately, the ideology at work here was arguing (though I'm sure my colleagues wouldn't have articulated it so bluntly) that an impoverished tongue equaled an impoverished mind, which equaled impoverished bank accounts for our students. It's an equation that the school accepted without qualms.

I'm not sure what is being seen in this debate—or, more specifically, this *lack* of a debate—about Appalachian dialect is that it *is* a dialect, with all that the term "dialect" entails. What I mean by this is that Appalachian language in this instance was not seen as reflecting a culture or a history. Instead, Appalachian speech, typified in terms like "I seen" and "we/they was," was perceived as reflecting a lack of education, an ignorance of correct English and by extension correct social values, which was by extension limiting students' economic and social possibilities. At least in our corner of Appalachian Ohio, this dialect wasn't being seen as a dialect. It was just a mistake.

————

When I was a master's student, I took a course on the history of the English language. One of our requirements was to conduct group research projects, the results of which we presented to the class. My partner and I chose as our focus French and Latin influences on early English, a topic I still find fascinating. However, one of the other groups chose to research Appalachian English, and their project had a greater impact on me than my own. What they found in their research was that many features of Appalachian dialect originated with Scotch-Irish settlers; they produced a list of Scotch-Irish terms, pronunciations, and grammatical features I recognized. For example, "You'uns," "redd up," and "piece (as distance)" were all familiar to me; I "in-joyed" things that others "enjoyed"; I'd never even realized that "the combination of need and the past participle of a verb" (i.e., "needs finished") was a regionalism.[8] The list went on. However, the presenters also found that the influence went beyond language. "Appalachian culture *is* Scotch-Irish culture," one of the presenters noted.

Well, damned if that didn't wake me up. This being roughly the era of *Braveheart* and the *River Dance* craze, the idea that Appalachian culture, Appalachian difference, could have such a cool explanation was thrilling to me. I have, however, come to believe that this statement about Appalachian culture, while understandable, is too simplistic. Simplistic, first and foremost, in that it risks overlooking the high degree of diversity and the varied influences permeating aspects of Appalachian culture. As Stevan R. Jackson points out, "Of all the stereotypes that haunt Appalachia, perhaps the most deceptive is that Appalachians are a homogeneous people with a single cultural heritage."[9] Sociological work has demonstrated a wide variety of cultural influences on aspects of Appalachian culture such as traditional crafts, music, and dance. For example, methods of traditional basketry can be definitively traced to the Cherokee, and that prototypical Appalachian musical instrument—the banjo—is African in origin, as are certain aspects of clog dancing.[10] However, linguist Michael Montgomery has noted that, while enough variations in language occur across the region to "justify the plural designation Appalachian Englishes," elements of the Scotch-Irish influence can also be found in multiple parts of the region.[11] In other words, the Scotch-Irish are not the only root influencing Appalachian language, but they are a widespread one.

Again, while micro-regional variations of language and culture do exist, and while cultural influences other than that of the Scotch-Irish are undeniably rooted in Appalachian peoples'

languages and identities,[12] I'm intrigued by the possibility of a
potential link, a linguistic thread working its way throughout different parts of Appalachia. Lyons states that a shared language is
one of the central tenets around which a people can be defined,[13]
making the importance of language to culture and identity difficult to overestimate. Sharing language, on its surface, is an easy
means by which to build shared identity; this conception has been
both recognized and coopted in recent years by groups wishing to
use "English-only" movements to exclude speakers of other languages in the United States.[14] (I'm guessing that the English touted
by English-only enthusiasts bears little relation to some of what
I've heard up in these hills.) But what about when the shared language is not recognized as being shared, even in various degrees?
In other words, how can we build identity around a shared language when we don't know that we share it, or why, or where it
comes from?

———

For the longest time, I had no way of thinking about our language
other than as incorrect or as a weird and somewhat undesirable
accent. When my dad would ask, "You'uns ready tuh git movin'?"
or when my mom would decide the dishes "needs worshed"—for a
long time I had no concepts by which to think about this way of
speech or its implications. It got marked off when it showed up in
school writing, I knew that. I also knew that we were, in US geographic terms, northerners. The distinction between North and
South remains a reified separation in both our history and modern
identity politics, but as a multigenerational Ohioan, it wasn't one I
was personally in any way confused about. Ohio (Uh-hi-yuh, as I
hear it pronounced) was a northern state; we had ancestors in the
Union Army to boot, though I've since learned that participation
in the Union or Confederate armies was also not clearly

determined by geography. Regardless, it was a bit of a shock when I stumbled on a recording of Sheila Kay Adams, a storyteller from North Carolina, who *sounded like us*.[15] Perhaps her language was ours dialed up a notch, but I could still hear it. It sounded extremely similar to some of my southeastern Ohio family members. (When Sheila Kay, telling the surprisingly funny story of a neighbor's funeral, cried out "Irvin! You got to come on down to the house an' help me git Amos up off'n the floor!" I could of swore I was hearin' my great-aunt Nova, who was born, raised, and lived her whole life in Monroe County, Ohio.) It was an experience that gave me some pause. Sheila Kay was from North Carolina, so she was southern . . . did we somehow have southern accents?

My conclusion, drawn after a good deal of research and reflection, is no, we do not have southern accents. Because me, my family, and my neighbors may sound a bit like speakers from North Carolina, but honey, *ain't a one of us southern*. What we are, in southeastern Ohio and in western North Carolina, is Appalachian. Whether we recognize that linkage, or not.

———

While not much good has been said about Appalachian language even in those regions where it is somewhat more recognized *as* a language (as opposed to a mere series of linguistic mistakes), one early attempt was made to lend it some social prestige. As Kim Donehower has noted, the early twentieth century witnessed the first wide-scale attempt by outsiders to romanticize mountain life, but on the dominant culture's terms. Essentially, Appalachian culture became defined, mostly by northeastern "culture professionals," as "representative of . . . 'pure' Anglo-Saxon culture," a belief bolstered by the idea that "Appalachian dialect is actually some form of 'Elizabethan English.'"[16] While I will be considering the implications of this misrepresentation later on, for now I only want to mention a few of the ways I find it troubling. Perhaps the least relevant to my current topic is the conflation of "Anglo-Saxon" culture and "Elizabethan" English. (I'm picking a linguistic nit here. The English language, by the reign of Queen Elizabeth I, had little to do with the English of the Anglo-Saxons, courtesy of the Norman Conquest. So, no "Anglo-Saxon" culture would have been speaking Elizabethan English.) But I am also disturbed by the easy ability of outside quantities to define our heritage, while ignoring the histories and experiences influencing that heritage. If the history of the Scotch-Irish and other Celtic groups demonstrates anything, it's that their history with Anglo-Saxon, and later English, power dynamics is not pretty or pleasant. To be defined, particularly to be mis-defined, in terms of that group is disconcerting, as a brilliant example of the power of the dominant group to influence identity and definition.

However, describing Appalachian English as somehow more deeply Anglo-Saxon than other variations of English is an assertion that is troubling in another important way: it is essentially wrong. Montgomery has demonstrated that "the Scotch-Irish contribution [to Appalachian English] . . . is much more substantial (in terms of number of features), broader (in terms of diversity of features), and deeper (in terms of the level of structure) than the Southern British or English one is."[17] This last point, about there being a deep structural linkage between Appalachian dialects and Scotch-Irish ones, is significant here because the links in surface vocabulary are much weaker. Montgomery explains that grammar "is more stable across generations and therefore easier to track historically" than terminology is. In fact, a great deal of Appalachian vocabulary was "actually born in America,"[18] though the reason for this is still a thread linking our language to the Scotch-Irish: linguistic creativity was something of a cultural trait. The documentary film *Mountain Talk* includes interviews with Appalachian residents regarding their language. Gary Carden, who is both an interviewee and the film's narrator, summarizes the history of his own Appalachian English:

> The Scots-Irish brought an early form of English, and many older words and expressions remained in mountain speech long after they dropped out of mainstream English . . . but many new words and expressions were invented here . . . . Older forms of English form the basis for mountain talk, but languages continue to develop, even in isolation. The seclusion of mountain life nourished the Scots-Irish talent for improvisation. Every community quickly developed distinctive dialect features, and new words and expressions.[19]

The Scotch-Irish didn't bring individual words so much as the interest in language that led to a development of new ones. Carden also notes that this creativity and uniqueness is "one of the delights of mountain life," which seems to me like something academia should promote rather than obscure.

Because when the cultural roots of Appalachian English are thus obscured, we lose access to important information that holds the potential for helping us shape and fight for our identities. How might my community college colleagues and my students have responded to the idea that the language they were earnestly working to "eradicate" was spoken in the grammar of William Wallace?[20] But here's the thing: they couldn't respond to that idea because *they couldn't see it.*

Lee Smith, in her essay "Southern Exposure," describes being told by a "northern" friend that she "ought to take speech lessens" to get rid of her "southern accent," something she refuses to do because maintaining her accent is a "political decision" against linguistic prejudice.[21] It's a decision I support. But this essay appeared in a collection titled *Talking Appalachian.* Although the book's introduction acknowledges varieties of Appalachian dialects, including those in what many would think of as the North, Smith's contribution hits on a commonly made correlation: Appalachian, essentially, equals southern. Lee Smith is a spectacular writer, and she absolutely has the right to describe her own language any way she pleases. What worries me is the wider correlation made by people who will simply assume that southern and Appalachian are the same thing. Sure, it's a political decision to maintain your language when your language is a recognized part of your heritage. But Ohio isn't southern. When the popular imagination conflates being southern with being Appalachian, we have less access to claims of cultural identity. The result being that talking like your grandma did isn't a heritage here, it's just repeating her mistakes.

This isn't to say that nobody in northern Appalachia sees it as a culturally relevant region, or that something like the Banned Terms Project couldn't have happened in a place where Appalachian-ness is more taken for granted, as it can be in Central and Southern Appalachia. But I can't get past that my colleagues, all of whom had degrees in the humanities and interests in campus multiculturalism, didn't seem to have seen what they were doing in terms of cultural denigration.

I believe that a greater understanding of linguistic history, especially when elements of it are shared across what we tend to think of as regional boundaries (North-South), can matter for how we construct identity. In fact, while Michael Montgomery's perhaps best-known work on Appalachian dialect examines language use specifically in east Tennessee,[22] his later work has also cited Alan Crozier's point that the greatest Scotch-Irish influence on Appalachian dialect occurs in western Pennsylvania[23] . . . in other words, in the North. Scholars have long pointed out that, when approached with respect, shared language has the potential to help people see themselves and their communities positively. Only, that is, if we can recognize what it is that we share. Language never operates in a vacuum; it connects us with our histories and ways of living, thinking, and interpreting the world.[24] I don't want to make language, specifically the degree of Appalachian dialect that I or any other people are perceived as having, the ultimate factor in how "Appalachian" a person can or can't be. Yet language is a factor; understanding and respecting language can be key to whether we also understand and respect the stories connected to it. Amy D. Clark describes language, stories, people, and place as intertwining to create her own "voiceplace."[25] I want *all* the peoples of Appalachia to have the chance to examine and share their own voiceplaces, no matter how much or how little these may sound alike.

Ultimately, language issues are some of the most well-covered ground in Appalachian literacy/rhetorical studies. Yet, that doesn't mean that an understanding of language issues or their influence on identity have filtered into the educational system. The Banned Terms Project showed me that a wider acknowledgement of Appalachian language and its validity has not happened, or at least not everywhere.

Chapter 3

Celtic Rhetoric

I'm sometimes surprised that, given the social disdain they face, Appalachian dialects haven't died out. It's a tenacious feature. I recall a presentation at the 2014 Appalachian Studies Conference describing a study that found third-generation out-migrants, who had themselves never lived in Appalachia, still showed some of the same basic linguistic features. Some still referred to the mountains as "back home," even though they had never personally lived in them.[1] Yet while I think language is an important factor in discussing Appalachian rhetoric, being maintained by and helping to maintain the rhetorical system, forms of spoken language alone are not the whole story I want to tell here. To explain this linguistic survival leads me to the more extensive features of its rhetorical origin. Specifically, I wonder if Scotch-Irish, and in a wider sense Celtic, rhetorical influences have a role to play in making such preservations occur and of making preservation itself something of a regional social value.

"Celtic" identity is a bit of a troublesome descriptor, as it has been coopted to support everything from white supremacy to the so-called inherent violence of Appalachian people.[2] These views are alike in seeing Scotch-Irish influence in Appalachian identity as a) about biology ("real" Appalachians are Scotch-Irish) and b) a concrete and absolute determining factor in people's views and behaviors (because they are Scotch-Irish, they act in particular ways). Of course, these ideas are too simplistic, even dangerously so. They erase cultural diversity while also presenting culture as immutable, even biologically ingrained. I wish to do neither of these things. However, the concept of Scotch-Irish or Celtic influence as part of Appalachian regional history is a strong one. My interest is in exploring that influence, what it might look like, and how it might emerge in examples of rhetorical writing and communication.

To begin with, the terms "Scotch-Irish" and "Celtic" themselves deserve greater explanation, specifically because both have been defined in different ways to support different agendas. My use of the term "Scotch-Irish," a term that other authors have sometimes used interchangeably with the terms "Scots-Irish" and "Ulster Scots," refers specifically to a population of Scottish Protestants who "migrated in the early 1600s to Northern Ireland, and then migrated onward to Colonial America during the years 1717 through 1775."[3] The Scots of Scotland shared some degrees of commonality with the Irish in terms of folk culture, with "Scot" being an early blanket term for inhabitants of both Ireland and Scotland,[4] and a great deal of mutual migration occurred between the two island nations up through the medieval era. However, the reasoning behind the 1600s emigration of Scotland Scots to Northern Ireland is significant to the story of both nations. Both countries endured patterns of invasion and colonization since at least the 1200s. By the late 1600s Scotland had (like England) begun serious religious reformations toward Protestantism. In a move calculated to "ensure the future pro-British attitude of Ireland," an attitude based largely on religion, some forty thousand of the poorest Protestant Scots were transplanted to Northern Ireland, to lands previously confiscated from the native, Catholic Irish by the English government.[5] While the term "Britain" is often intended to reflect the participation of England, Northern Ireland, Scotland, Wales, and Cornwall in a united society, I tend to use "England" to refer to the political and cultural power center that had, to varying degrees, dominated those nations. The politically motivated movement of Scots is known to history as the "Plantation" of Ireland,

and the people who took part became known as the Scotch/Scots-Irish or Ulster Scots, Ulster being the region of Northern Ireland in which they predominately settled.

Upon arrival in Ulster, they discovered similar dynamics to those they had left. Arable land access was as much the province of the Anglicized elite in newly colonized Ulster as it had been in Scotland.[6] Also, they were caught in a cross-fire with the dispossessed native Irish, now competing against the Scotch-Irish for dominion over their homeland.[7] After a few generations, many Scotch-Irish continued on to the New World, where they became an early population of European immigrants into what we now call Appalachia.

This is in general the population to which I refer when I discuss the Scotch-Irish influence in Appalachian rhetoric and culture, but I also refer to something larger than these few thousand individuals. I refer to their participation in and preservation of a rhetorical and cultural system that I'm calling Celtic. The terms "Celtic" and "Gaelic" are, most specifically, linguistic terms, to describe a particular population of speakers who, though dwindling in numbers, remain concentrated on Western Europe's "Celtic Fringe" of Ireland, Scotland, Wales, and Brittany. Though many of the early immigrants in Appalachia hailed from this region, I have found no evidence for the survival of the Celtic/Gaelic language in Appalachia in any substantive form. (I do have one minor caveat to this. I learned as a child to say "Hi" in a way I've yet to hear pronounced outside of the region; it sounds somewhat like "Hoyt." About a year ago I found my way onto the Irish Gaelic page of the Mango Languages website, which allowed me to listen to pronunciations of common Irish Gaelic phrases; I learned that there is a formal hello and an informal hello in that language. Imagine my delight when I clicked on the "Informal Greeting" icon and heard the speaker say what sounded an awful lot like "Hoyt!" I cannot definitively say this is a linguistic hold-over, but I can't say that it ain't, either.)

There are reasons for why Celtic language holdovers don't seem evident in Appalachian language; specifically, that most if not all of those early immigrants were speaking English as a primary language by the time of their arrival. Yet that doesn't mean that alternative influences weren't present in other aspects of communication and identity; speaking English didn't necessarily mean that people were "Anglicized" culturally or rhetorically. Reaching back to early examples of writing from Europe's Celtic Fringe, I have found that there were discernable differences between the styles of the surviving Celtic texts and their English counterparts. This is particularly true for texts from Ireland, which is the origin of most of the surviving (and translated) texts I've found. In looking for ways that the Scotch-Irish may have influenced Appalachian rhetorical styles, I am to a degree linking rhetorical influences from Scotland with those from Ireland, influences not entirely severed by the imposition of national, religious, or even linguistic borders. Huw Pryce, the author of *Literacy in Medieval Celtic Societies*, argues that Ireland, Scotland, Wales, and Brittany can be seen as similar in literary and cultural outlooks. While not uniform, these countries bear enough similarity to justify studying them together as culturally "Celtic."[8] Helen Fulton also identifies the term "Celtic" to describe a group of linked yet marginalized cultures.[9] In exploring the development of a cultural and rhetorical style in Appalachia, I rely on the concept of Celtic as a cultural descriptor, rather than strictly a term to denote speakers of the Gaelic language. I am thus using the term "Celtic" as a descriptor for the specific rhetorical culture of the Scotch-Irish.

This reliance is based on the idea that the Scots shared at least some rhetorical/cultural similarities, despite times of conflict, with the native Irish, from whom many of the extant resources on Celtic rhetoric stem. However, perhaps the strongest argument *against* defining the Scotch-Irish in particular as culturally Celtic comes from the more recent disputes in Northern Ireland. Religious and political differences between the largely Protestant Scotch-Irish and the largely Catholic Irish have, in the twentieth century, been so great as to result in extreme acts of violence. Also, some of the descendants of those Scotch-Irish Protestants still living in Northern Ireland have, in modern times, worked to define themselves as culturally more Anglo/English than Celtic, due to their religious differences from the rest of Catholic Ireland. However, Padraig O'Snodaigh, in his book *Hidden Ulster: Protestants and the Irish Language*, defines these attempts by the Scotch-Irish to "anglicize" themselves as a more recent phenomenon, born of deliberate work by an Anglo-elite to disrupt potential commonality between the Catholic Irish and Protestant Scots. O'Snodaigh notes that the initial Scottish settlers and Irish natives recognized their similar cultural heritages, a state that contributed to shared cooperation despite religious differences.[10] As the original intent of the Plantation system was to subdue and convert the Catholic Irish to Anglicized culture, religion, and loyalty, this cooperation essentially undermined English authority. In response to the threat of Scottish and Irish social/political/cultural intermingling, the ruling class deliberately (and successfully) imposed laws and educational curricula to create identity tensions between the two groups. O'Snodaigh cites the 1870s as the approximate point by which Scotch-Irish Protestants as a group began to disavow their Celtic identity, a point by which many of those who would become the early Appalachians had already emigrated. Therefore, the Appalachian Scotch-Irish would have had far less exposure to deliberate attempts to alter their cultural identities.

The situation between the countries of Europe's Celtic Fringe is, in a way, a situation similar to what I perceive in the American states of Appalachia; despite lines demarcated on a map, and perhaps even in people's minds, connecting threads—connecting rhetorics—may be there if we look for them. Like Ireland and Scotland, which share geographic similarities, Appalachia's hills in West Virginia are connected to the hills of Tennessee, of Pennsylvania, of Southeastern Ohio. The peoples are not identical, nor were the Scotch-Irish the only element influencing cultural/linguistic development in these regions. Yet, to reiterate Jackson, they were influential.[11] While work has been done on the ways this influence plays out linguistically, far less has been done to consider how the Scotch-Irish have shaped wider rhetorical patterns, in terms not just of the words people use but *how* they use them and what they use them to do.

It's a tricky undertaking, certainly, to boil anything as complicated as a rhetorical system down into distinct statements. Consider what follows, then, to be by necessity tentative and mutable. However, my research uncovers what seem to be prominent features of Celtic rhetoric, features that I've gleaned by reading both original Celtic texts (in translation) and the relatively few works on this subject I've found by modern scholars. Celtic rhetoric doesn't have the same glamour as Greco-Roman or medieval English, and it is made more difficult to examine because there are fewer surviving written texts. However, the historians and rhetoricians who are focusing on Celtic studies have done admirable work in bringing these features to light. What I haven't previously seen, however, is a specific connection drawn between this rhetorical history and Appalachia.

The rhetorical features I discuss below, which are also features that I believe figure in Appalachian rhetoric, are based in the works of other scholars but are ultimately my interpretations and therefore subject to my subjectivities. But something I think I've inherited from this Celtic rhetorical tradition is an ability to be comfortable with my individual subjectivities and to accept them as just that.

So . . . let me just show you what I'm thinking.

———

Some Features of Celtic Rhetoric:

Ethos is built through demonstrating humility and group identification; speakers/writers must identify with the audience,
not set themselves above or apart from them.[12]

Conceptual boundaries are blurred: for example, the differences
between the speaker/writer and the audience, between
modes of communication, and between past and present are
less distinct than in modern, mainstream thinking.[13]

Narratives (often non-linear) demonstrate the speaker/writer's
process of thinking about a subject; in other words, stories
show how one has come to knowledge or belief, without
overtly insisting on similar beliefs from the audience.[14]

The process of thinking/coming to knowledge is often shaped by
family and place-based experiences, with the assumption
that the audience will also value these as sources of knowledge.[15]

Rhetoric is less about arguing in favor of specific ideas as it is the
preservation of mindsets and ideals, connections, and
consensus about general values.[16]

———

Loyal Jones describes in his book *Appalachian Values* a set of
social ideals he sees as prevalent in Appalachian culture, including, among other things, humility. While Jones's project is something many have questioned because of its potential for

oversimplifying and concretizing a singular definition of Appalachian culture, I include it specifically because the type of humility he describes is something I've witnessed in my own regional context. It is a humility that means not groveling nor necessarily lack of pride, but rather a hesitance to present oneself as separate or, most certainly, as better than others. A friend of mine said something not long ago that I think captures the dynamic perfectly: *I may not be better than anyone else . . . but that sure as hell don't mean anyone's better than me.* It is bad manners, in other words, to hierarchize ourselves. Humility is a social value that seems to set us apart from much of mainstream American pop culture, which, from what I can tell, seems to equate success to fame, to notoriety, to being the wealthiest, the most talked about. The most distinct.

In teaching one of my recent rhetoric/composition courses, I asked my students to read editorials written by local citizens who were debating the repercussions of fracking. My students that time around, all of whom hailed from outside the region and none of whom identified as Appalachian, seemed confused by what they were reading. My students noted that the editorials all "made a big deal" about how long the writers' families had lived here; as a reader, I took it for granted that this kind of connection with place was demonstrating credibility, rather than its lack. However, these editorials also included a plethora of phrases seeming to indicate the writer's uncertainty or tentativeness; the writers were frequently emphasizing that their arguments were "only" their own opinions, while they also seemed quick to emphasize their own rural backgrounds, sometimes even foregrounding their lack of formal scientific education. "They really don't have much credibility," one of my students said, and although I was thrilled that he was attempting to analyze ethos, I think there was something fundamental he missed as a cultural outsider. There was a reason these editorials were written the way they were, and it was not, I suspect, because the writers hoped to *not* be listened to.

I'm using humility-as-ethos as a means to begin considering what medieval Celtic rhetoric was like, and by extension its fingerprints in the modern Appalachian rhetoric I've encountered, because I think it serves as a useful threshold by which to understand the purposes and appearances behind this complicated system. And it is complicated. I see a very real visual connection between the complex designs of Scotch-Irish-style quilts and the complexity of the interlaced patterns in Celtic art; perhaps this connection can also be extended to the complexities of Celtic rhetoric and mindsets. In these, conceptual borders were much less distinct than what tends to be the case in cultures influenced by Greco-Roman civilization. For example, in Celtic ideology matters spiritual, physical, and imaginative were intertwined.[17] In other words, "natural" and "supernatural" were not necessarily separate concepts; the spiritual world was expected to mix and merge with daily life, just as the past was expected to exist within and assert influence on the present.

————

One of my earliest memories is of my mother reading Laura Ingalls Wilder's *Little House in the Big Woods* to my brother and me. I can remember her telling us at certain points that this was a bit like what life would have been like for my grandfather and his father, both of whom had grown up in the "Old House" that was then decaying softly in our front yard. And in some ways, it wasn't so different from our own experiences. For example, I learned about trundle beds, not much different from the foldout mattress where we sometimes slept on the living room floor—the easiest room in the trailer to keep warm in the winter. But even though we had conveniences neither Laura Ingalls Wilder nor my great-grandparents had dreamed of, knowing something about their lifestyles was seen as important. There was something worthwhile in thinking about and talking about what life was like for the generations that came before. Later, my mom started writing these down; she typed out the stories she knew about different ancestors and glued them into clear plastic boxes with accompanying heirlooms—the tintype picture of my great-great grandfather in his Union Army uniform, the mason's pin my great-great-great grandmother wore when she traveled here alone from further East. The past wasn't dead and gone; it was right there, in stories we could read and tell, pictures we could see, recipe books we could follow. Quilts we could wrap ourselves in.

Yet even the parts of the past that were dead stayed with us. I was very young the first time I was told, in perfect seriousness, that the Old House was haunted. Not in the sense that something frightening or vindictive dwelled there, but rather that a presence remained—something that more than one of my family members felt and that at least one had seen, in the shape of a white-garbed woman assumed to be my late great-grandmother. Sharyn McCrumb describes ghost stories, like childbirth narratives, as a form of stock story among Appalachian women,[18] something that connects the tellers to each other, to the places they've lived, and to the people who have come and (not necessarily) gone before.

Mom and I went to see my grandmother's cousin Dorothy in Monroe County a couple summers back. Grandma had passed on by then, but we took her sister, my great-aunt Nova, with us because she and grandma had grown up with Cousin Dorothy like sisters. Over the course of the afternoon, more women arrived, all cousins of some stamp or another, all eager to see Nova and my mother and, I was surprised to learn, me. I'd never met most of them, or if I had it was when I was too young to recall—the Carpenters are spread out across the hill country in several states, and it isn't often so many of us are in the same place at the same time. But every one of them wanted to know me, seemed to think it was *important* to know me, because I was family, and there were stories to tell. We sat around a table and in easy chairs eating hickory nut cake and drinking coffee, while the women told family stories. More than one of these involved not just the living, but also the dead. I learned which of these relations had lived in haunted houses, and I learned which of their various relatives or neighbors they thought was doing the haunting. I learned which ancestor's husband was terrified of ghosts and how she used to sneak outside and throw stones against the wall to scare him, until he would yell for his wife to come and protect him. These cousins of mine wanted to hear my stories about the haunted dorm I'd lived in as a student, which had no connection with the family's ghosts, but still, as a haunting story and a place story, mattered. Of course, I'm not saying all Appalachian people believe in ghosts. I know plenty who don't. But the stories I've heard, and the interest I've seen people have in telling them, not to frighten, but almost to reassure, makes me wonder: the past and present, the spiritual and physical—maybe it's only in some people's imaginations that these things were ever distinct at all.

———

Those of us who teach English and writing know that words matter, but I'm not always sure that many others realize how much. There seems to me to be the oddest sense in this country today that words don't really "mean" anything if we don't want them to; "words" and "actions" are taken as two completely separate things, with only the latter being truly important. It's not a way of thinking that would have been recognized by ancient Celtic societies. One of the most revered social positions in the medieval Celtic social structure was that of the *filid*, the poets, who were not poets in our modern sense. Rather, the *filid* were a learned rhetorical class, who played a "semi-sacred role in interpreting the world,"[19] serving as what we might consider simultaneously poets, priests, historians, lawyers, educators, and jurists. For them, no event was unique or unconnected; the complex nature of the relationships between events, peoples, and nature could be articulated and understood through the stories told by these multi-skilled wordsmiths. It was those who were skilled with rhetoric, with communication, with language, who were thought to be able to see, to judge, to teach. The stories that were taught and told were what established normalcy and perpetuated those norms in society, teaching people what to expect and how to behave. Words and stories were seen as so important that the ancient Irish people were "fascinated by the power of language *to shape reality*" (italics mine).[20] Those educated to possess a rhetorical ability this important didn't limit the scope of that power to singular roles in society.

That these roles—teachers, judges, historians, entertainers, poets, priests—were considered compatible, indivisible, and equal in itself indicates a difference between Celtic societies and the hierarchical, categorized ways of thinking common to the modern United States. We don't look to historians to judge the present, we don't look to poets to make law. Modern life in this country is dominated by what Kentucky writer Wendell Berry calls "specialization" thinking[21]: each of us enters a box and looks to others whose "job" it is to provide anything outside it. We do one thing; to do anything else is to overreach. Think about the uproar, for example, when actors or artists comment on politics. "Do your job and stay out of things that don't concern you" seems to be a popular response on social media in these situations. What that response overlooks is the degree to which things outside of our specialization *can* concern us. Celtic ideology recognized interconnections to a far greater degree, even to the point that the Celts have been described by one scholar as having tortuously complicated mindsets.[22] More than one scholar of Celtic thought has drawn correlations between this emphasis on interconnection and the complicated interlaced patterns of Celtic art and script.

Yet by playing all of these roles, by seeing these interconnections and telling the stories that mattered to people, Celtic rhetorician-poets created and maintained cohesion among a somewhat scattered rural populace.[23] My sense is that in this system, humility functioned to create ethos because the general goals of Celtic rhetoric were different than those of Greco-Roman academic rhetoric. The classical Greco-Roman rhetoric that has influenced academia's modern sense of the term held that "Rhetoric was, first and foremost, the art of persuasive speaking."[24] Persuasion and argumentation developed as the end-goals for rhetoric in the urban polis of Greece and the Mediterranean.[25] Meanwhile, being Quintilian's "good man speaking well" meant standing apart, up above the fray. Likewise, in a formalized political system in which swaying public opinion could create very real effects, distinguishing oneself from one's opponents could reap political rewards.

However, this was not necessarily the case in ancient Celtic societies. Because the social and geographic worlds of the Celtic Fringe were so vastly different than those of the Mediterranean,[26] the rhetoric that developed here was also vastly different. Here, life revolved around rurality rather than urbanity; rhetorical communication developed less as a means of changing minds and more as a means of encouraging cultural unity among a "decentralized, rural"[27] people. As social and political authority was more diffused than in the urban polis, being able to connect with and be listened to by wide groups of people meant identifying closely with as many of them as possible. While hierarchies existed in Celtic societies, the surviving texts don't seem to emphasize these in terms of giving particular characters or voices greater worth. I imagine that to achieve a hearing among people who need not, if they chose, listen to you at all, humility would be quite a good approach. (Seriously, I don't know who all would've listened to Plato's Socrates where I'm from. His whole rhetorical success depended on people being actually willing to stand around and play his game of "dialogue," which only ended after he'd gleefully painted his opponents into a rhetorical corner. In a graduate class I took on classical rhetoric, I remember asking why none of these people simply refused to engage with Socrates. My discussion partner, who was non-Appalachian, seemed to think I was confused about what was happening in the text. Maybe I was. Personally, I think if I were in one of those conversations, the second Socrates started acting like he had all the answers and I was an idiot . . . I would've walked away and made sure to *never see him again*. I live out in the country; we got room to do that here.)

Significant, though, is what that rhetorical humility hoped to achieve. And it is here that I see perhaps the greatest defining feature, and differentiation, of what I think of as Celtic rhetoric from that of the Greco-Romans: it was communication not intended to establish argumentative dominance or individual rightness on particular points or ideas (goals that might well create offense between speakers), but rather to create group cohesion, to preserve traditional lifeways and mindsets that could benefit life in a particular environment. As Michelle O'Riordan notes in her book *The Gaelic Mind and the Collapse of the Gaelic World*, "the poets arrived at a language and a mode of expression which articulated . . . the nature of their relationships" with each other and with the world; it was a world of relationships, both current and historic, in which "everything is related to previous mythical or historical events."[28] Within this web, the power of words to shape reality was well understood by Celtic rhetoricians; language was used "for teaching and normalizing [through] stories and poetry."[29] The rhetorician's ethos assumed great importance in this system, but through identification rather than self-promotion. A successful rhetorician in a Celtic context "had to identify . . . with the vocabulary, the values, and the symbols [of the audience] . . . to reaffirm as

much as to transform."[30] In other words, the role of the Celtic rhetorician required blending in more than standing out, as the ultimate goal was the preservation of something far wider than the
individual self: a worldview of vocabulary, values, and symbols.

Among the understood symbols was the power of story, of illus-
tration, as the means by which people learned to think and act in
particular ways. As forms of rhetoric and writing were not necessarily subject to separation and hierarchizing, narratives retained
their centrality; they never became defined as a lesser form of communication, even for academic and legal purposes. However, the
form stories took was not identical to the modern academic mode
of narrative writing; specifically, these narratives were "in no way
concerned with presenting a chronological account."[31] This blurri-
ness on the subject of chronology may be a cardinal sin in academic narration (I'm thinking of how many times I've lectured my
own students on the importance of transitions as chronological
guide-stones for readers.) However, these at times nonlinear narratives worked particularly well in the Celtic system, as they allowed
for an emphasis on individual thought processes and experiences,
more so than on audience expectations. This emphasis, in turn,
allowed for the conveying of ideas and values without what might
be called *pushiness*. Rhetoricians were able to use stories to educate, to preserve, in a way that maintained humility and did not
force acceptance onto the audience. *This is how I think, and this is
why,* the subtext of a story might say. *You may choose as you will.*

For example, the *Senchas Mor,* one of the surviving Irish legal
texts of the medieval era, starts with an illustrative story about a
mythical/historical figure's conversion to Christianity;[32] in fact,
legal writing was considered to be tightly linked with literary and
historical writing (those blurred boundaries, again) to the point
that many such surviving legal documents contain fictional and
mythological narratives within the law tracts.[33] The purpose of
these stories was not to establish rules to be followed in every case

(avoiding ideological pushiness, again), but rather to establish precedents, to illustrate how the experiences of historical, fictional, or mythic jurists could illuminate the experiences of modern ones. Significantly, the stories themselves weren't even necessarily focused on particular laws; instead, they "centre on *the process of judgment itself*" (italics mine).[34] It was the experiences of others within a shared cultural and geographic context that taught how to think and act individually, as each individual's thoughts and actions in turn maintained tradition and unity. To figure out what to do, people were invited to see what others had done in the past.

In considering Celtic rhetoric as an influence on the Appalachian rhetoric I grew up with, I think that there are viable linguistic, stylistic, and conceptual linkages, but I also think there is a direct link between the cultural values that Celtic rhetoric sought to maintain and those prevalent in Appalachian culture. Among the values that emerge most strongly for me include those that privilege history, family, and place—concepts that are presented as not necessarily distinct from each other. I take as a strong example of this emphasis the twelfth/thirteenth-century Irish text *Acallam na Senorach*. The *Acallam*, a form of narrative depicting conversations between characters, does what many other Celtic texts have done in that it "navigates the spaces between fiction, identity, and history,"[35] building Irish identity through the use of Irish rhetorical traditions. But what I find significant is the sense of identity the text is building: it is an identity inextricable from the land and the people's history with that land. Sarah Connell identifies an oral and literary tradition of using language and narrative to construct an identity "built around claims that the people and the land of Ireland are not separate or separable," a tradition that "would prove influential for centuries to come." In emphasizing continuity between peoples and places, the rhetoric itself did a great deal to ensure the preservation of this social value. Time was not, in other words, a factor that separated or changed peoples and places, but rather one that wove them more tightly together. The narratives of the *Acallam* and the *Senchas Mor* encouraged their audiences to see themselves in terms of place and history, to essentially create the continuation of these identities by continued emphasis on these dynamics. By demonstrating the characters' links to the land, the *Acallam* encouraged listeners/readers to share that sense of identity. We as the audience are invited to identify with the characters as they describe the connections between themselves and the land. I believe that in modern Appalachia, there's plenty of us who would.

I anticipate some pushback against my interest in exploring linkages between Appalachian rhetoric and that of the medieval-era Celtic Fringe. Some might worry that by linking the influence and survival of this style of rhetoric to its compatibility with rural, decentralized societies, I'm negating the experience of urban Appalachians. That is not my intent. Because preservation is one of the rhetorical values I'm highlighting here, this style of rhetoric could thrive in any location, provided that the people continue to see preservation and perpetuations of these values as linked to a positive sense of identity. If being Appalachian for you means telling your grandchildren the stories your granny told you, and if you see being Appalachian as a good thing to be, then you're gonna tell them stories no matter where you live. And, given the results of the study I mentioned at the beginning of this chapter, at least some Appalachian out-migrants do. I remember a conversation I had with scholar and native West Virginian Todd Snyder, who was moving to New York to take up a faculty position. "I'll be Appalachian wherever I go," he said, and that statement has stuck with me. For me, "Appalachian" is about, ultimately, the stories we tell ourselves and how we tell them. Far from denying anyone else's stories, I'm just trying to historicize some of those options.

Also, some might say my connection of this modern rhetoric with medieval Celtic roots does Appalachia a disservice, by perpetuating the sense of Appalachia as somehow frozen in the past. Not long back, I was discussing *The Hunger Games* with a group of junior-level composition students.[36] I was disappointed but not really surprised to find that few of them realized that Katniss Everdeen, the female hero who little girls around the nation were dressing as for Halloween and taking up archery in hopes of emulating, was meant to be an Appalachian woman, the latest in (for me, anyway) a storied history of strong Appalachian female heroines. My students simply didn't get it. But what was enlightening for me was how one student explained why Katniss's Appalachian identity wasn't self-evident: "*The Hunger Games* is set in the future," that student said. "I don't really think of Appalachia in terms of the future."

I can understand this viewpoint, and I can see how it is problematic. But I wonder too why such a connection with the past is framed as something negative. The "past," that time frame in which Appalachia eternally exists, is presented as both something distinct from the present and something shameful to be stuck in. Kim Donehower warns against approaches to Appalachian culture that advocate "preservation": "Preservationist projects that seek to turn rural communities into museums essentially ensure that those communities cease to exist, as no one actually lives in a museum."[37] Good point. (Although to be fair, I know plenty of people who'd live in museums if they were allowed to, because museums are awesome.) But what if we have, as I think we have, inherited from those Scotch-Irish settlers a way of life in which culture, and our means of communicating culture, is inextricable from preservation—where preservation, in essence, forms the root and purpose of our rhetoric? Where a tradition of narratives provides precedents by which to evaluate the world and our relationships? Where "the past," as others think of it, as something dead and gone, doesn't exist because it lives in us, while the dynamics that shaped our past continue to shape us today? The ideas and identities preserved by our rhetorics have arguably helped us to survive, to create connections between events, to endure, *to continue*, in troubled times. It has kept alive with me good people and a good land. And I'm at a loss to see the shame in that.

———

One stereotype of Appalachia that seems to run across the board is that of the rugged individual, of people who hew a hard life for themselves, by themselves, and prefer it that way. When I say it runs across the board, I mean that it isn't an idea held mainly by outsiders—it seems to be what many Appalachians believe of themselves. Loyal Jones, for example, includes self-reliance on his list of Appalachian cultural values.[38] However, Snyder has written a brilliant analysis of the means by which individualism, as a social value, has played into the agendas of extraction industries (primarily coal companies) to discourage Appalachian workers from seeking assistance to fight for better working conditions. In other words, I'm not disputing the existence of individualism as a social value. But I'm curious about what this emphasis on individuality means to the possibilities of building wider Appalachian group identity, the peoplehood that Lyons argues is necessary to the fight for rhetorical sovereignty.

What I am wondering is whether surfacing how individualism works in our rhetoric, where it comes from and what its limits are, can help create threads of recognition between widely spread Appalachian peoples. I think many of us would at least recognize the social value for individual self-reliance; it's something politicians play on when joyfully offering to cut our social service programs. Really good, decent people wouldn't need them anyway; they would earn their own way without "help." It's only the lazy and worthless who seek such "handouts." Of course, this ideology overlooks many harsh realities, entirely obscuring the experiences of the working poor, yet it's an ideology that continues to receive support within the Appalachian region. Yet what if more of us knew, consciously, how much our rhetorical history also values community? The narrative-based rhetorical tradition I've described allowed for individualism, by emphasizing people's individual voices and processes of judgment. Yet it also encouraged communal values and assent over confrontation by its very unwillingness to emphasize categories and exploit hierarchies. Can we, in other words, critically explore the limits of individual self-reliance as a positive social and rhetorical value?

Helen Fulton describes the field of early Celtic literature as "diverse yet coherent."[39] This concept of simultaneous diversity and coherence is made possible by the style of rhetoric in which individual perspective is emphasized; yet demonstrating humility—the recognition of other possible perspectives—creates the credibility that makes one worth hearing in the first place. It seems to me that a wide-scale critical understanding of this rhetorical tradition and its affordances is yet to occur in the Appalachian region.

Warren Hofstra notes that while "understanding individualism is critical" to an understanding of the Scotch-Irish immigrants to the United States, it is "[n]ever absolute, the individualism of the Scots-Irish was alloyed with the ever-present authority of community and the need to live together not only among themselves but also among diverse peoples in various political contexts,"[40] within what was often a disconnected, rurally settled population. Perhaps there is an opportunity to create cohesion, group identity, *people-hood,* and all the potential political and social benefits therein, including rhetorical sovereignty, through the simultaneous respect and allowance for individual identity. In other words, I think when we have the chance to see and hear each other's stories, we can learn to recognize links and value differences, in ways we never will if they are never shown.

My overarching interest is in the ways a greater public understanding of this rhetorical heritage could move us closer to attaining rhetorical sovereignty and the social privileges that sovereignty entails. If Appalachian dialect, as well as the wider system of traditional narrative rhetoric, were more widely understood to be in part an outgrowth of Celtic rhetoric, perhaps this understanding could lead to increased social respect. Teachers and students could develop a greater interest in what happens when Appalachian peoples open their mouths or put pen to paper.

I don't mean by this that I want us to simply latch on to a mainstream cultural fad involving Celtic heritage, though one certainly exists—there's a reason the term "Celtomania" became popularized in the wake of *Braveheart*'s box office success, after all. My interest in surfacing one of the heritages of Appalachian rhetoric has less to do with what that heritage is than the mere fact that it exists at all. I remember how I felt reading Geneva Smitherman, the wonder I felt in thinking that an AAVE speaker could, in a sense, be speaking something of an ancestral language hundreds of years and thousands of miles removed from its land of origin. I was fascinated to learn that there is a reason for AAVE discourse to be what it is, a reason that does not equate to ignorance, a reason that is, for me, innately respectable. To speak in the voice of my ancestors, even just a little, means something to me. And, given that the discussion on dialect and world Englishes has only grown in the academy, it means something to many educators, as well.

Yet again, I think there's room to expand Appalachia's visibility in this conversation. For example, Katherine Kelleher Sohn, whose book *Whistlin' and Crowin' Women of Appalachia* was the first I had ever encountered to focus on Appalachian students' experiences with academic literacy, recalled witnessing professors at a conference in Nashville, Tennessee, mocking their Appalachian waiter's accent. These are teachers, she believed, "who, if asked, would probably pride themselves on their multicultural awareness."[41] Yet they failed to recognize Appalachia as part of the very multiculturalism they hope to advance. I think the same dynamic was at play in the Banned Terms Project, which intended to help students succeed, yet completely overlooked the ways in which their home dialect could be a relevant part of their identities. For this reason, if no other, I think a greater awareness of our cultural roots is important in mainstream and academic contexts. However, it's important, too, for us, as Appalachian peoples, to have the opportunity to explore the cultural heritages that not only influence our language and ideals, but could also link us together on a much wider scale than we've yet experienced. There is power in community, in identity, which I think our rhetorical styles can recognize, even if we have not consciously considered it ourselves.

CHAPTER 4

Celtic Rhetoric in Appalachia

Having investigated Celtic rhetorical traditions, I want to look at the ways these facets linger in some of the present day's Appalachian rhetoric, in terms of what they might look like when they show up in regional writing. As someone who has struggled to understand the requirements of academic writing, I am deeply invested in understanding why the ways of writing that seemed normal to me also seemed to diverge from what is required in writing classrooms. In fact, Appalachia is no stranger to writing classrooms. I've discovered that there is more scholarship available on the subjects of Appalachia, writing, and rhetoric than one might think.

In researching this book, I've come across multiple explorations of these themes. Katherine Kelleher Sohn's *Whistlin' and Crowin' Women of Appalachia* is an early, and still deeply important, example. Published as a 2003 article in *CCC* and as a book in 2006, it was one of the first focused, scholarly examinations of Appalachia and issues of writing or literacy. Sohn's interest was in the ways Appalachian women utilized the academic literacy they gained in college in their social and professional lives afterward. This was followed by Jennifer Beech's 2004 *College English* essay, "Redneck and Hillbilly Discourse in the Writing Classroom: Classifying Critical Pedagogies of Whiteness," in which Beech asked Appalachian students to closely examine the discourses that dominate mainstream definitions of Appalachian identity in unfair ways. In 2007, Sara Webb-Sunderhaus's "A Family Affair: Competing Sponsors of Literacy in Appalachian Students' Lives" appeared in *Community Literacy Journal*, considering how family served to aid or inhibit Appalachian students as they learned academic discourse. Also in 2007, the book *Rural Literacies* was published, in which Kim Donehower authored a chapter examining the ways mainstream and academic discourse have influenced negative Appalachian stereotypes. Even closer to home, Nathan Shepley's 2009 *Composition Studies* article, "Places of Composition: Writing Contexts in Appalachian Ohio," compared the experiences of an Appalachian student and a non-Appalachian student in a composition course at Ohio University, demonstrating that the experience of the Appalachian student wrestling with academic discourse was significantly different in complex ways. More recently, Amy D. Clark and Nancy M. Hayward's edited collection *Talking Appalachian* (2013) and Sara Webb-Sunderhaus and Kim Donehower's edited collection *Rereading Appalachia* (2015) have continued to extend the conversation surrounding Appalachian dialects and literacies.

My purpose in this rundown is to demonstrate not just what I've seen in the scholarly literature, but also what I haven't. The above consider predominantly the ways mainstream or academic discourse shapes Appalachia and/or the experience of Appalachian students encountering academic writing—certainly an important focus and well-worthy of extended inquiry. However, what I want to focus on to a more extended degree is how cultural history influences the ways students' home discourses and identities can be written, not just how they encounter academic writing.

Let me dwell for a minute on one article in particular. Though I didn't mention it above, Erica Abrams Locklear's "Narrating Socialization: Linda Scott DeRosier's Memoirs" appeared in the 2007 issue of *Community Literacy Journal*. Like Webb-Sunderhaus, whose article "A Family Affair" appears in the same issue, Locklear focuses on the culture clashes Appalachian students can encounter in academia; her views (and those of DeRosier, an Appalachian memoirist whose work she evaluates) tell me something important about the current gap in this area of scholarship.

Locklear's textual analysis of college professor and memoirist Linda Scott DeRosier's published writing highlights the ways that college education distanced her from her sense of Appalachian identity. DeRosier, upon entering college, "increasingly learns that her Appalachian way of being contrasts with accepted ways of being in the academic community," a contrast that DeRosier manages via "a constant obsession over passing for 'normal [. . .] not hillbilly.'"[1] While DeRosier later became troubled by her own desire to assimilate, she continued to value her ability to use mainstream discourse, as it allowed her to write the memoirs wherein she challenged negative Appalachian stereotypes.

This article echoes Webb-Sunderhaus's piece in significant ways. Locklear notes DeRosier felt compelled to disavow her Appalachian identity when she attended college, much like the students in Webb-Sunderhaus's study. As with Webb-Sunderhaus, Locklear leads me to question why there must be such a difference between academic and Appalachian identity. Did DeRosier believe her memoirs were only possible via the standardized writing discourse she learned in college? Did her publishers? Could such work be written in any other way than with the rhetorical conventions of the academic mainstream?

By focusing intently on how non-regional discourse interprets Appalachia (such as with Donehower) or on the ways by which Appalachian students adapt to academic or mainstream discourses (as with Sohn, Webb-Sunderhaus, and Locklear), what remains open for exploration is the inner-life of Appalachian rhetoric. (Coincidentally, what I'm doing here is something I was taught to do as part of the academic discourse training I gained in graduate school: I'm looking for potentially productive gaps in the existing scholarship. It's training that has allowed me to notice that this here is a *big* gap, with room for many more explorations than just mine.)

While these authors are doing unquestionably important work in bringing scholarly attention to the subject of Appalachia and considering how best to open mainstream and academic discourses to Appalachian students, I want us to think, too, about the rhetorical literacy these students bring with them to the classroom (perhaps even subconsciously), where this literacy comes from, and what it means. What I have gained in this exploration is a greater sense of myself and my identity as shaped by rhetorical forces that have a much longer history than I'd ever realized. I feel more connected to the people who came before me, and I know more of what I want to pass to those who come after, and *how* I want to do so.

The connection of writing with mainstream (or otherwise non-Appalachian) rhetoric is something worth challenging, for academics and for Appalachians. By surfacing an Appalachian rhetoric that can and has been written, specifically in the service of memoir-writing, I find greater strength to contend that my Appalachian identity is discursive, is writeable in a way that isn't often considered, and that has a value I want to see recognized and advocated. Appalachian rhetoric need not distance me from the writing classroom. Rather, it can make me part of it.

———

As I've mentioned, there have been Appalachian people writing in (and being written about in) the academy and mainstream society for some time. And much of this writing is done, or at least attempted, in mainstream or academic dialect, both in terms of language and rhetorical choices. What I want is something different: I want to look at how Appalachian people might write when they're writing for themselves and other Appalachians, when they're writing in ways that seem fittin' for these occasions. I'm going to try, in essence, to eavesdrop on Appalachian writers, writing their own stories.

What I'm listening for is not necessarily about language choices. There is writing that "speaks" in an Appalachian tongue, certainly, but I'm not sure this can be the primary factor by which to examine a text's rhetorical choices, for particular reasons. For example, some Appalachian writers have never written in their home dialects, particularly if their writing instruction comes primarily from post-WWII public schools. In these cases, the teaching of writing and the teaching of standard English have often overlapped, to the point that a more standardized English has become no less the default language of writing here as in the rest of this country. This is, more or less, my own case; I never really learned to write in anything but standard English, nor did I get much experience speaking my home dialect in academic contexts. Even now, I find myself having to think, when attempting to demonstrate my home language for my students, about what I would say or how I would say it if I were pretty much anywhere but in a classroom. Sometimes, when I hear myself saying something in a way I think of as Appalachian, I force myself to remember it for future reference. (A while back, I was walking past the road construction being done outside my apartment. Because it's a construction site, it turns into a mud hole when it rains, which it was doing then. One of the workers saw me, and politely apologized for the layer of mud I was getting on my shoes. "I grew up on a farm," I assured him, "'Is here ain't nothin'.") It doesn't come naturally to me in a schoolroom, nor on a blank page.

I've found that a nervousness about written language among Appalachian writers correlates with a deeply running set of social judgments about Appalachian English, making its appearance a potential sore subject for some speakers and writers. Katherine Kelleher Sohn agonized over how to transcribe the language of her Kentucky interviewees in her ethnographic study, coming to the decision to standardize in order to protect them from these judgments:

Appalachian ethnographer D.E. Walls defends his choice to regularize language by stating that the "attempt to use the vernacular misfires in one of two directions. Either it confuses and slows down the reader or it reduces the mountain characters to little more than ignorant, comic fools. I had no desire to do either" (xiii). Though all language systems are rule-governed and legitimate, I wanted my audience to hear these women as intelligent beings who had something to whistle and crow about; I did not want someone judging them as "ignorant, comic fools."[2]

What is problematic is that this places the burden of "sounding" intelligent on the speakers, rather than holding the dominant-dialect audience accountable for their own prejudices, for assuming intelligence can only sound one way. Sohn describes this realization in her later essay "Silence, Voice, and Identity among Appalachian College Women," asking herself "How could I claim to honor their language and continue to challenge language attitudes and prejudices if I edited the very language that defines them?"[3] However, Sohn was also faced with her Appalachian interviewees' desires to *be* edited; upon showing her the edited transcription, one participant, Jean, "edited her transcript even further, saying that she did not want to sound like a 'hillbilly' to anyone else reading the transcript."[4] This linguistic sensitivity "occurs when outsiders' attitudes are internalized by insiders trying to 'better' themselves."[5] In other words, it is from outside, rather than within, that correctness is defined, which says something about the distance Appalachia has to go to attain Lyons's definition of rhetorical sovereignty: the US as a whole seems nowhere near accepting regional varieties of "correctness." Nathan Shepley encountered a similar attitude regarding dialect in his interviews with Matt, an Appalachian student, who stated:

My accent's probably a lot worse than I let on. I do—it's not that I'm embarrassed of where I come from or who I am. It's just that people perceive you differently if you've got this, you know, southern drawl thing going on. So, it's trying to conceal that sometimes 'cause you don't get taken seriously, and I've experienced it before. People just don't, you know—they're not into what you're saying.[6]

Matt also lays the ultimate responsibility not on listeners (to confront their own linguistic prejudices) but on speakers, including himself, to prevent such an awkward situation from arising.

This attitude, however, is not shared by all Appalachians or academics. In transcribing her interviews with an Appalachian Ohio woman, sociologist Rosemary Owsley Joyce chose not to edit for standardization, deciding that "It seems to me a heightened form of snobbery not to use the vernacular, a subtle way of saying 'You talk funny, and rather than embarrass either of us, I will clean up your act and make it sound like it should—like me!' Pure ethnocentrism!"[7] Also, in one of the most famous examples of Appalachian autobiography, Loretta Lynn emphasized that when she agreed to write a memoir, she insisted on control over her language, but not so that it could be standardized:

The first thing I insisted was that it sound like me. When all those city folks try to fix up my talking, all they do is mess me up. Like the way I pronounce the word "holler." That's our word for the low space between two mountains. City people pronounce it "hollow" but that ain't the way I pronounce it. This is *my* book. Instead of using Webster's Dictionary, we're using Webb's Dictionary—Webb was my maiden name.[8]

It's difficult, then, to make any definitive statement about how Appalachian peoples feel about language because opinions (and the reasons for those opinions) are so mixed. Therefore, what I'm looking for is what goes on in writing below the linguistic surface. In other words, I'm looking to see how Appalachian rhetoric can be more than just the shape and sound of the words we use.

Specifically, what I'm looking for are rhetorical conventions that the authors themselves may or may not be aware of using; they may simply be writing in a way that "makes sense" for them. But what is it that makes sense for Appalachian writers? It is, for me, both a very personal and a very social question, and again, not something I'm trying to answer for everyone. Are the ways in which I feel drawn to write, to express myself, and the ideas I feel compelled to express just some individual quirk? Are they just me being me, or are they something far wider; something that, in understanding, can help me understand myself and perhaps help other Appalachian writers understand themselves, as part of a culture?

I'm thinking here, again, of Matt, the Appalachian student in Nathan Shepley's study. Listening in on Shepley's interviews with Matt, it's easy to grasp that Matt's conceptions of himself are complex; he is aware of himself as Appalachian, to the degree that he self-identifies as such, which is itself an identity marker not all inhabitants of the region are aware of as an option—for many of us, there is no term for who and what we are, or at least no positive term. Matt *claims* Appalachia; he knows it is there to *be* claimed. Yet, what that identity means, how it is shaped and expressed, is something more complex and seemingly less known even to himself.

Matt's conceptions of Appalachian identity, as seen through his views on language, are certainly not simple: he is embarrassed by the language bequeathed to him through this cultural identity, having been taught that it is a "worse" way to speak, yet he is proud of his family and neighbors, who likely speak the same way.

However, what is of even more particular interest to me are the rhetorical dynamics that Matt doesn't seem to recognize himself utilizing, dynamics that he may not even label as particularly Appalachian, but that we can catch traces of in his classwork and interviews. For example, Matt notes that he could "more easily engage in class activities and writing if he could explore familiar subjects"[9]; the subjects he specifies are family and place-specific. He describes at length his grandfather as both an intelligent man and one of his (Matt's) own best teachers, though he explains that his grandfather's "intelligence was in things that applied to him, you know, gardening or farming or something like that. That was where it applied to him. It wasn't, you know—he didn't know about Shakespeare or Virginia Woolf or things like that. It didn't appeal to him. It wasn't useful in his world."[10] Loyal Jones has specified family and place as being central values in Appalachian culture; whether or not you agree with the validity of Jones's project, I can say this: these are values I recognize. Matt's grandfather, based on this description, could easily be my own. Pap's intelligence was ferocious, and he used it to adapt to his environment brilliantly. Having lost an arm in World War II, Pap designed and built for himself a peg that he could strap to the stump and therefore operate the strings on his banjo. He designed and built a mechanized fishing pole that he could operate with one hand. He found a way to plant seeds with a mechanized corn planter, so he wouldn't have to dig, then put down the dibble, then pick up the seed, then plant and cover the seed, then pick up the dibble again . . . as you can guess, that process would have gotten old, fast. Instead, he fractionalized the length of time something like planting a garden would take with one hand. He was also an avid local historian. One of my early memories is of him showing me pictures of the U.S.S. Shenandoah out of an encyclopedia and telling me about the crash site, which wasn't far from where we lived. We had seen a blimp that day flying along the interstate line, and in retrospect, I'm not at all surprised that, in explaining to me what a blimp was, he tied the concept to something local.

But as far as I know, he never read Shakespeare.

I have read, and love, Shakespeare, and I think Pap would've enjoyed the history plays. I doubt, however, that he had ever had the chance to think of Shakespeare as something that could have any relevance to his life and world and to me, that's a shame. Nonetheless, I don't think him any less brilliant for his lack of interest in classical literature. I posit that, as Matt suggested, part of my own Appalachian rhetorical inheritance is a value for applicable intelligence, the desire to talk, write, and think about (and thereby preserve) the knowledge that is "useful in [our] world"— usefulness that is, in this cultural context, linked inextricably with that which allows us to build and maintain place and family links.

Shepley notes that differing values seem to distance Matt from the writing assignments he is asked to do in class. For example, one assignment asked students to "pretend they were writing three letters to three different audiences in order to get money for spring break," to which Matt responds, "I would never do that. I would never be able to do that." Shepley considers a cultural value for self-reliance to be at the root of Matt's discomfort, making him unwilling to even pretend to be asking to borrow money. I wonder, too, if he was repelled by the idea of taking money, perhaps dishonestly, from parents or family to use on his own pleasure; I would have been. Matt had earlier mentioned his discomfort at his non-Appalachian classmates' cavalier attitudes toward "their parents' credit cards," a judgment he makes but also tempers with the olive branch of "I'm not saying that [all they do is party]."[11]

Perhaps this attitude toward money, family, and personal responsibility is, as Shepley suggests, rooted in Appalachia. If so, how is it formed and perpetuated? Matt's subjects and styles of communication could have bearing on this. I see, for example, a potential connection with Celtic rhetoric in the qualification Matt makes on judging his classmates, in softening the statement, keeping the emphasis on his own lack of perfect knowledge of his classmates' values. He may judge them, but he'll also point out that his own judgment isn't perfect. I'm interested in how deeply ingrained these concepts seem to be for him, how rhetorically bound they are with not just how Matt speaks/writes but what he speaks/writes about and why those topics seem valid. Unlike his discussion of his language, Matt doesn't describe this desire to write about family and place-based subjects as negative, or even necessarily positive, perhaps because it is simply something beyond those value judgments: it just *is*, it's how the project of writing makes sense. Matt wants to write about place and family as important subjects, topics that would be relevant and engaging to him. Perhaps they've been presented to him this way his whole life.

————

This desire to eavesdrop on Appalachian rhetorical conventions has a lot to do with how I chose which texts to eavesdrop on. My choices are, more or less, samples of autobiographical writing, as these are texts in which writers, in telling their own stories, are perhaps more likely to write in ways that seem natural to those stories, particularly for audiences with shared regional backgrounds. Think of it this way: if I'm going to tell you'uns about my life, I'm going to tell it in ways that make sense to me, particularly if I'm not conscious of how those ways conflict with those of the academy. I'm choosing for this analysis writers/speakers who are, to some degree at least, writing at home—who demonstrate that Appalachians can *be* at home with writing at all. As writers, they aren't necessarily trying to do things differently than what feels right to them. And it's this "home" writing that I want to explore, not least to show that writing "home"—writing Appalachia—on its own terms is possible.

However, my choice of memoirs as rhetorical texts may require some explanation. Are they? My gut answer to that question might be, "They are, here." But that is because of what I think of rhetoric as doing—specifically, I think of "rhetoric" as a means of creating, sharing, and understanding one's self and one's world through language. In analyzing memoir, I'm seeking to better understand what that world is for these writers, how they create it, and how they communicate it. Academically speaking, memoir is often considered the realm of creative nonfiction; in other words, it's more of an art form than a means of practical communication, and it doesn't necessarily seek to make any specific argument. I'm sure that some creative nonfiction writers would certainly define their works as artistic explorations, untethered by rhetorical purpose. Defining art versus rhetoric in and of itself would be an exhausting discussion, one I'm not proposing to have here.

Yet, the research I'm finding on Celtic ideology could do something to bridge the art/rhetoric debate. I am intrigued by a point that I came across again and again in my research of Celtic rhetoric: that of interlace, a desire to obscure boundaries or disconnections in favor of surfacing third spaces, unities. The religious life of Pagan Celts had this element ingrained. There was no Celtic deity of love or one of death in the Greco-Roman sense; rather, there was one goddess of both love *and* death, another of war *and* fertility.[12] Likewise, they drew few distinctions between concepts of narrative, poetry, or song—all were vehicles for the magic of language, a magic that allowed the world to be created and maintained.[13] For the Appalachian rhetorical tradition that I'm describing, the creation of a memoir could be both an artistic and rhetorical undertaking, its product simultaneously a work of artistic, literary, and rhetorical purpose.

This combination of purposes is perhaps more commonly seen in works of fiction. Sharyn McCrumb's Ballad novels nearly all examine fictionalized versions of historical events, including the

Civil War (*Ghost Riders*) and famous murder trials (*The Ballad of Frankie Silver*). McCrumb's novels repeatedly emphasize the power of the past to maintain or influence the present, to prevent the present or future from becoming "unpredictable."[14] Although at least some of the characters and situations in her novels are fictional, they also include historical events and real-life characters that keep the past ever present (so to speak) in the reader's mind, alive and capable of shaping current reality in ways we have to think about in order to understand or control. Likewise, Denise Giardina (*Storming Heaven*) and Diane Gilliam Fisher (*Kettlebottom*) use fiction, or in Fisher's case story-poems (any distinction between story or poetry not being dwelled on in her work), to educate readers about the West Virginia Mine Wars, using fiction to keep the focus of history on real lives, on people's lived experiences. In each of the aforementioned works, we see from multiple characters' perspectives and through their own voices how history has had real effects on the peoples and places of Appalachia. Therefore, each makes an implicit case that individual voices matter, that remembering the past matters, and that place can have much to do with who we are. In Sharyn McCrumb's novel *The Songcatcher*, an elderly Appalachian character named Nora is described as keeping careful records about her neighbors and community happenings. As the novel describes:

> For many years she had kept track of the families in the valleys, faithfully recording the births, the deaths, and who married whom. Even in her youth, the young people of Wake County had been moving away, called out of the hills by war or colleges, or the promise of better jobs in the cities. She knew that someday they or their children would be coming back, perhaps only briefly, but returning to look for the pieces of the puzzle of who they were. Sometimes they came to see her—these well-dressed strangers bearing in their faces the

echoes of their bloodlines. They would ask her about their roots, and she would always do her best to sort it out for them.[15]

History is being presented here as both personally and communally important to the shaping of Appalachian identity. Likewise, the gathering of these histories, not just one's own but those of neighbors, is presented as socially important and worthwhile.

Again, these literary forms, in the hands of Appalachian writers, are playing interlaced roles between fictional entertainment, literary art, historical analysis, and rhetorical argument. Though not writing fiction, the Appalachian memoirists I've read to some degree mimic these forms of boundary crossing, with their texts functioning as life stories as well as works of historical/cultural analysis and tacit rhetorical arguments for valuing the roles history and place can play in identity.

I'm wondering now if perhaps there is something culturally dependent in my thinking of rhetoric, and memoirs *as* rhetoric, in this way. Huw Pryce described early Celtic literacy as being used to foster native culture, specifically to preserve and transmit learning and lore.[16] My sense has always been that this is what memoirs, as life narratives, do: they are told (or written) to create and share a sense of one's worldview and to preserve that worldview. I think that memoir, therefore, can be a particularly relevant form of Appalachian rhetorical writing; recall Matt's desire to focus his classroom writing on his own experiences, as, in fact, the only way in which he would truly feel engagement and comfort in his writing. I don't see this as evidence of Matt's failure to distinguish rhetoric from creative nonfiction or to understand what is relevant as an academic subject, or as evidence of simple self-involvement on his part. Rather, I think he's responding to a cultural sense that personal stories are a good way to convey one's ideas and sensibilities; in other words, to write rhetorically.

I would note, however, that what Matt and I may be thinking of as "personal experience" and memoir could use some deeper examination. Matt wanted to write not only his own experience, but also that of family and neighbors. This is perhaps not the same as what might be defined as *personal* experience in other contexts. It is a definition of personal experience in which *I*, the person in question in the term "personal writing," might not appear at all, or at least may at times seem to take a back-row seat. Telling my stories means, sometimes, telling the stories that were told to me, whether or not they were about me at all. I don't think I'm the only Appalachian writer who defines other people's stories as part of my own.

I think memoir, whether oral or written, whether told from the teller/writer's personal perspective or not, fulfills a rhetorical purpose in the Appalachian tradition I'm describing: it draws connections, between people and with social values, and it puts us in our place, sometimes literally. It emphasizes that we, even as writers, are just one thread in a larger cloth that someone started sewing before we were even born.

———

A while back there was a wedding in the family. My great-aunt Nova's husband, Girdon, and his sisters Marcella and Cinderella got up to sing some of the old songs to the guests. The old style isn't so common anymore, certainly not outside the area. It's a throaty sound, where the goal is not so much for your voice to sound pretty but to sound strong. One of my mother's many cousins had brought his new girlfriend over for the event. When Girdon, Marcella, and Cinderella started singing in the old style, in that wonderful, harsh harmony of voice . . . his girlfriend laughed. She howled. She nearly fell off her chair, she thought they sounded so funny. Our cousin said nothing.

None of those three sang much after that. And our cousin married that girl.

Did I just write a memoir? In other words, is this part of *my* story? That's a bit of a complicated question, not least of all because it is, strictly speaking, a memory that is not my own. I am nowhere in the scene itself, which occurred before I was born. I had no influence on any part of it. I'm not even, by the definitions of mainstream nuclear family relationships, closely related to the participants (my great-aunts and great-uncle, my distant cousins by blood and by marriage). But I would say that this is, for me, a memoir; it *is* personal experience. Because it's a story that I've been told through family channels, one that has had an effect on how I define the world. On what I value . . . and on behavior that I don't. Specifically, I learned (or perhaps better to say, had reinforced) the value of respect for elders and the devastating cost of disrespecting cultural history. I learned that this disrespect need not come from the outside: the girlfriend, and later wife, was also local. As such, I learned something about the concept of internalized oppression, long before I ever learned there was a term for it.

Perhaps the question I should ask is, in writing (or in having been told) this story, am I engaging in rhetoric? This is a question that might have a somewhat clearer answer, depending on one's point of view. Because, in fact, if I am to ask the question from a traditional first-year college writing definition of rhetoric, the answer could be no.

It's no real secret that much of what is considered rhetoric in academic contexts descends from specifically Greco-Roman rhetoric. Think, for instance, of the textbook *Classical Rhetoric for the Modern Student* by Edward P. J. Corbett and Robert J. Connors. It's an excellent rhetorical text, but as the introduction makes clear, the origin of "classical" rhetoric is the urban *poli* of Greece and Rome. And Greco-Roman rhetoric takes the form, quite often, of "instances of formal, premeditated, sustained monologue in which a person seeks to exert an effect on an audience."[17] Already, this definition problematizes the informality, abruptness, and spontaneity of the Appalachian narratives I grew up with. My mother's telling of the wedding story was not planned, nor was it formal, or packaged with a stated moral or thesis (although I could tell pretty clearly what exactly my mother—the teller—thought of that laughter, the loss she felt, from that thoughtless act of humiliation, in not hearing that singing like she once did.) Greco-Roman academic rhetoric is, as Aristotle described, at root the art of persuasion. While Corbett and Connors note that this definition can be expanded to include both argumentation and exposition, it seems clear from any informal survey of composition textbooks that argumentation in particular reigns supreme as the purpose of academic rhetoric. Yet it's hard to describe the telling of this story as argument in any academic sense.

Argumentative writing has a fairly definitive form and definition in many first-year composition textbooks. Written arguments revolve around a discernible, relevant issue, with an identifiable thesis making a clear claim on the issue that the audience is (hopefully) going to be convinced to agree with by the end of the essay.[18] Some even go so far as to instruct that "argument is always grounded in reason,"[19] a concept with deep Greco-Roman philosophical roots. By this definition, personal or family experience and ethos take a backseat unless they can be quantified, made logical . . . that is, if they appear in good academic writing at all.

I wonder, then, what this can mean for the reception of our stories as rhetoric. I don't think the wedding story would pass as an academic argument; as I said, I wasn't asked, overtly and formally, to accept a claim about an issue as the audience for this story. (I'm likewise often uncomfortable asking others to accept *my* claims.) I could guess pretty easily what my mother took from it, and what I'll even go so far as to say that she hoped I'd take from it, but I don't know that it was a hope that could even be articulated at the time: it would have felt pretty strange for her to preface the story with, "Here's what I want *you* to think about this." What happened was something subtler. I could see what she thought and why, and I could take it from there. It didn't even need explained why something like this, revolving as it did around valuing heritage and respecting family elders, was an "issue" worth addressing. It just was. So if what we have in Appalachia is a rhetoric, it ain't necessarily a Greco-Roman one.

The study of women's rhetorics in particular has done a great deal to expand accepted definitions of what rhetoric is and what it does, beyond the narrow limits of the Greco-Roman tradition. As Joy Ritchie and Kate Ronald note in the introduction of *Available Means: An Anthology of Women's Rhetoric(s)*, while "women have often written in unprivileged or devalued forms such as letters, journals, and speeches to other women," a renewed examination of these texts as rhetoric has created "an expanded definition of rhetorical form."[20] Therefore, by asking us to fit Appalachian life-writing (what I am, for lack of a better term, calling memoir) into that definition, I am doing nothing new. I'm just stretching the already well-worn definition a little further. Maybe, to maintain my metaphor, I'm quilting together memoir and rhetoric into an interlacing pattern, for what I see as an Appalachian rhetorical purpose: by analyzing these texts rhetorically, seeing what it is I can learn from them to better explain my own sense of culture and its shaping influence on identity, I hope to present a picture of my own thinking, laid bare. Because while I find myself uncomfortable with the academically rhetorical concept of thesis-based argument, I can make a purposeful demonstration of my process of thinking about how Celtic rhetorical heritage has shaped my understanding and experience with Appalachian rhetoric. Because it is my hope that my thinking will, in some way, hold value for more than just me.

CHAPTER 5

Writing an Appalachian Rhetoric

In order to explore more fully how the rhetoric I'm describing works, I propose to listen in on memoirs by two authors: *An Enchanted Childhood in Raven Rocks* by Elsa Crooks Harper and *The Way It Was* by Della Grace Kindness. These texts are similar in context, making them beneficial and problematic to my proposed eavesdropping in similar ways. Both are, for me, local texts, in that they were published in small, regional print runs for small, regional audiences: Crooks Harper by Raven Rocks Press and Kindness self-published by the author, with copies printed on request. Both are for local audiences, advertised through regional newspapers and word of mouth. Both the authors are known to members of my extended family network, which is how I learned of their existence in the first place. These kinds of texts, while not unheard of, aren't exactly common in my neck of the woods, though. The style of rhetorical discourse I'm investigating remains largely an oral tradition. I asked my own grandparents more than once to write down some of their stories, to no avail; "Well, just let me tell you," was the response I got, time and again. For whatever reason, writing didn't seem to them to fit the stories they had or how they wanted to tell them. My grandmother tried once to write down the story of the time her little sister got new shoes, but they were accidently burned up when the teacher at school set them beside the stove to dry on a rainy day. She made it about half a page, then quit. Writing simply wasn't something they were comfortable with for telling others about their lives. It is this conceptual separation between storytelling and writing that I hope, even in some small way, to undo. Because there are many other grand-parents, aunts, uncles, children, *people* out there in the world whose stories we will never hear unless we can read them. And because, to my eternal shame, there are so many of my own grand-parents' stories I've forgotten.

It does, however, happen on occasion that someone local puts their stories to paper, and those instances are instructive. I know of other similar texts (at least one of which is a memoir that has been simply typed out on loose-leaf paper, with copies made at home and distributed to interested readers), all of which are simi-lar in their composition and intended audience. I don't know how many Appalachian memoirists achieve or perhaps even aim for a national audience (Loretta Lynn's *Coal Miner's Daughter* being an exception, although it was written with a coauthor). Perhaps if nothing else, J.D. Vance's *Hillbilly Elegy* will encourage even more Appalachian people to take up their pens. However, I suspect part of the reason why these memoirs remain localized has to do with the effects of writing Appalachia as a discourse. When commit-ted to the page, these narratives don't necessarily look like what the rest of the country may be used to in a memoir. So what does our Celtic rhetorical inheritance *look* like when you put it on a page? Maybe nothing like what you'd expect. Or be willing, even able, to read as I think it's intended. We can write Appalachia, in other words; I'm less certain that everyone knows how to read it. With this in mind, let me sift through some of the Celtic rhetori-cal threads I brought up previously and see if I can find them in my quilt.

———

Rhetoric is less about arguing in favor of specific ideas as it is the preservation of mindsets and ideals, connections, and consensus about general values; the process of thinking/coming to knowledge is often shaped by family and place-based experiences, with the assumption that the audience will also value these as sources of knowledge.

In 2012, Stephen Fry filmed the BBC documentary series *In America*, in which he traveled the fifty states seeking the roots of both regional differences and similarities. In Kentucky, he stopped in on an informally organized, public bluegrass music session. One of the players, after a demonstration of his banjo pickin' (three-fingered style, he explains, like Earl Scruggs), discusses the Scotch-Irish origin of his musical style. He ponders the wider implication of what playing this music means for him: "I would say that it, it runs deep in your blood and it becomes a part of you . . . and you feel the land, you know, in your heart." I find it interesting that for this young man, Scotch-Irish music is a means of "feel[ing] the land . . . in [his] heart," specifically because that music was born an ocean away from the land it's helping him connect with. My sense is that this connection comes from a rhetorical tradition that uses expression, including music, to tie oneself into place, into, as he says, the land.

In her article "Writing on the Land of Ireland," Sarah Connell makes the case that Irish texts like the *Acallam na Senorach* effectively linked identity with geographic space; in other words, that the text worked rhetorically to "merg[e] their bodies with the land."[1] This is achieved textually by the narrators demonstrating their knowledge of place-based traditions: "the *Acallam's* author is able to show how the people of Ireland have shaped the land in which they live—and how the land has also shaped them. . . . [through knowledge of] *Dinnshenchas* [place-name lore] and genealogies, knowledge of the land itself and of the people who inhabit that land."[2] The text becomes a "synthesis of narrative traditions, people, and physical geography"[3] that preserves the connections between the people and place of Ireland, connections that Connell argues were particularly important to articulate at the time of the

Acallam's composition, during the early waves of Anglo-Norman colonization.

My suspicion is that something similar can happen when Appalachian writers put pen to paper, in that these same ideas—a value for connection between peoples and places, and the preservation of those connections—play an important, if not always surfaced, role in their rhetorical choices. In other words, I wonder if we aren't writing ourselves into place, too, using the stories we've made and been told.

For example, in Della Grace Kindness's memoir there is a chapter titled "Blooming Grove Community." Here Kindness details a "special section of Oxford Township" where "probably the first settlers had discovered a grove of trees, maybe in the springtime when they were in full bloom."[4] I am always struck, in this passage, with Connell's central point about the role *Dinnshenchas* (place-name lore) plays in the *Acallam*,[5] a role it also seems to play in this text. Kindness's chapter continues to provide a verbal map of the region, in rather mundane detail. For example, we learn:

> At the crossroads stood a one-room schoolhouse . . . . Although the farms adjoined, the houses were not close together . . . . Besides the school there were two churches in the community: Saltfork Baptist Church which, from what I heard, was quite prosperous and well-attended, and Pisgah Church which was located toward Route 40 . . . everyone around gathered up apples from their own individual orchards and brought them to Doc's mill.[6]

For her readers, the specifics of these details may hold little meaning; some of the places she describes, such as the one-room schoolhouse and Doc's mill, no longer exist. What I also find significant is that, before explicating these details for her readers, Kindness prefaces her chapter with the statement "I only know these things I write about from what I have heard from my parents and brothers."[7] Kindness herself was raised in the nearby Antrim community, not Blooming Grove, where her family lived before her birth. However, that doesn't make Blooming Grove any less significant when she tells her life story. She describes Blooming Grove because it was part of her *family's* place-connection, something she perceives as important when telling her own life stories.

So why explicate these (perhaps ponderous) geographic details, when they are not even part of her own narrative, her own life story? Because, I would say, for her they *are* part of her life story, exactly because they are part of her wider familial connection with a place. They are also part of her rhetorical purpose in committing these accounts to writing. Kindness not only expounds on the historical minutia of a disappeared farming community, she also emphasizes that this knowledge about places, even if that knowledge is at a remove from her individually, is *important*. By demonstrating her knowledge, Kindness demonstrates what it means to belong to a place, a form of identity that, in writing her memoir, she encourages preserving.

While I do not know if Kindness made these rhetorical choices consciously in the writing of her memoir, I do think Elsa Crooks Harper shows some rhetorical awareness of her views on language, place, and identity. She begins her own memoir not with herself or her family's history, but with place: "[b]ooks grow," she tells the reader, and "[t]his one is the outgrowth of my enchanted childhood in a unique area of the state of Ohio, an area that has long been called the Raven Rocks, since large flocks of ravens were known to have gathered here."[8] (Notice again the emphasis on place-name lore.) In other words, her book, her writing, is nourished not just from her life, but specifically from a particular place's influence on her life. By making these her opening sentences, Crooks Harper is emphasizing an interconnection among self, communication, and place that is both sophisticated and, by Connell's measure, a rather traditionally Celtic way of looking at the project of rhetoric. While Connell notes that the *Acallam* demonstrates a process of textually tying together people and place, Crooks Harper explains a tradition of locals writing themselves quite literally into the landscape of the Raven Rocks; people "tied ropes onto the trees above, and swung over the edge, anchoring themselves while they managed, with difficulty, to carve or paint their names."[9] I get the sense that what Crooks Harper is doing, textually, is writing her own name on the landscape that has, as she acknowledges, written on her. However, it is not her own name she wishes to inscribe; as an Appalachian author, Crooks Harper has many names to write.

Ethos is built through humility; the speaker/author must identify with audience, not set herself apart.

Both Elsa Crooks Harper and Della Grace Kindness take steps to emphasize a sense of humility in their writing that might seem counterintuitive to the authors of autobiographies. It might be said that committing one's life experiences to writing, and taking the added step of publishing that text for others to view, is by nature an act of pride, or at least the belief in something exceptional about oneself, something others will find admirable or worth considering. Yet both these Appalachian authors seem to work intentionally to undercut any sense of self-exceptionalism, by redirecting their readers' attention to the wider contexts they share with others: by emphasizing, that is, family, community, and place. Both are writing to audiences they conceive of as connected either by ties of place, of blood, or both; these ties are emphasized rather than down-played in the creation of an individual's authorial voice. Kindness's memoir begins in fact with no mention of herself; rather she begins with a meditation on the importance of remembering one's forebearers with "love, honor and respect,"[10] followed by several pages on the history of her family's roots in the region of her upbringing. Crooks Harper is even more direct in offsetting her own authorial voice; she states on the first page that the content of her book, and by extension her identity, is not solely hers but rather the compilation of "experiences with my own family . . . early childhood friends, and [with] neighbors in that world of quiet, peace, love, and beauty."[11] She creates credibility and authorial identity not as exceptional among her audience but as solidly one of them, with, like most of her audience, family roots in the region and a home that she emphasizes was not *grand*, but rather *good*.[12]

It is precisely because of this humility, this identification, that she can attest "I have never been ashamed of my upbringing."[13] By avoiding pride, she by extension avoids shame. As Paul Lynch explained regarding the rhetoric of St. Patrick, ethos in this way is built not by being special or distinct, but rather the reverse: by identifying with "the vocabulary, the values, and the symbols"[14] of the audience, which in this context, ethos values both humility and individual judgment. As these authors make clear, their viewpoints are their own, but these viewpoints are also not exceptional; rather, they reflect many others.

Narratives (often nonlinear) demonstrate the speaker/writer's process of thinking about a subject; in other words, demonstrating how one has come to knowledge or belief, without overtly insisting on similar beliefs from the audience.

However, I also perceive something of a paradox in these examples of Appalachian rhetoric, a paradox that offsets their attempts to decentralize their authority within highly individualized styles of narrative. Let me explain what I mean by that. Appalachian peoples have something of a reputation as storytellers. A book of critical essays on the works of Appalachian writer Sharyn McCrumb is even titled *From a Race of Storytellers*, the "race of storytellers" in question being the Appalachian peoples from whom McCrumb draws much of her inspiration. Yet many of the stories I see from Appalachian writers like McCrumb, and even memoirists like Crooks Harper and Kindness, don't overtly try to enforce interpretation, to tell the audience what the "point" of the story is that they should take away. In fact, Crooks Harper looks at it like this: "Not all of us see beauty in the same paintings, the same poems, or the same music. We each tend to bring to any form of the fine arts our own feelings, past experiences, or appreciation. However, . . . I hope the reader will find something [in this book] which will captivate."[15] Despite her later assertion that her homeland and its stories have much to teach,[16] Crooks Harper is pretty well satisfied to leave it up to the readers to take what they will from her stories. Instead, what we see in both Crooks Harper and Kindness are a collection of stories designed to illuminate the development of their lives in particular places, with the tacit understanding that the reader may take from this process and the author's conclusions what they will. The effect sounds strikingly similar to that of the *Acallam* and other early Celtic texts, in which the rhetorical emphasis was placed not on a distinct thesis but rather on demonstrating an individual's process of judgment or coming to knowledge.[17]

It is a difficult balance these writers achieve, in emphasizing that their words are "just their own opinions/ideas/experiences" while also recognizing and giving credit to the families, communities, and places that have shaped these opinions/ideas/experiences. Something that I suspect helps them achieve it is the specific form of storytelling and narrative structure the writers utilize. My experience with academic writing textbooks, specifically those geared toward community college writers (with whom I have most of my experience as a student and a teacher), is that they are usually pretty clear on how one should write a narrative; academic narratives, or at least good ones, are organized chronologically. Description can be utilized, but it plays a secondary role to the chronological flow of events; sometimes, it's presented as an entirely different mode of writing (as in, for example, the popular *The Sundance Reader*). To a large degree, it seems to me that academic narrative writing is inextricable from "event"; in other words, narrative itself, even when somewhat grudgingly accepted as a possible form of rhetorical composition, is intended to tell a specific story about a specific happening, in order to more fully persuade the audience of the correctness of the writer's specifically stated thesis. That, however, is not the style of storytelling happening in these texts—not least in that sometimes the stories don't have a central event at all. While I'm sure that not all Appalachian writers, were they to set down their own memoirs in writing, would compose them the same way, I'm interested in the style I'm seeing in these Appalachian autobiographies, styles that I think can be historicized culturally.

In that light, what is particularly interesting about the collections of stories in both Crooks Harper and Kindness is that they aren't necessarily chronological, not focused on particular events, and are at times taken over by description. Crooks Harper, for example, follows her own discussion of community quilting parties by inserting a description of the appearances and joys of farmhouse porches (a discussion that she likewise interrupts with a sudden and detailed description of her family farmhouse's rain barrels). Likewise, Kindness quite often follows family stories and experiences with detailed descriptions of the layout and geography of her childhood community; in fact, she sandwiches her description of the layout of the Blooming Grove farming community between a story about her brothers and her recollections of the family horses, Doc and Dan. Distinctions between modes of writing like description and narrative, as well as the rules for their organization, certainly don't seem to follow textbook guidelines.

In fact, these memoirs defy chronological organization from the first pages. Both authors begin their memoirs not with their births or anything else so easily described as an "event," but rather with depersonalized discussions of places. Crooks Harper begins with interspersed descriptive prose and poetry about the Raven Rocks, including not just a description of the geographic details but also historical details of the region's development ("Little Piney Creek, through the ages, had slowly but surely worn down the soft rock, leaving a harder rock which has formed caves and overhanging roofs"[18]). She then describes phases of human interaction with the land, from Native peoples through miners and farmers who live in dependence on the land itself. Her notations about the place are, as she specifies, not only her own; she intersperses her own knowledge and experience with that of others (such as "my mother could remember when the overhanging roof extended from each side so near that one could step from one side to the other"; and the story of when "my father and a neighbor decided they would explore the Bear's Den"[19]). It is through these loose gatherings of description and story that she writes her own family's roots in the region. Kindness likewise begins her memoir with place, but in the context of a more distinct description of her family's genealogy. Her introduction begins with the statement "A George family was living somewhere in Massachusetts in the 1700s"[20]; she then skips forward to a description of the first ancestors to settle in southeastern Ohio in the early 1800s, a family line that has remained in the region ever since. She concludes this combined family-place genealogy by describing her memoir as "a true story about a family, a town, and the people who lived in and around this small community in Ohio known as Antrim."[21] What she describes as "a story" is in fact what many might call a random collection of anecdotes, descriptions, documents, poems, and photos, rather than a linear narrative of events.

What to make of this, then? Are Crooks Harper and Kindness simply bad writers? I would argue not; rather, what we can see in these texts is an effect of the individual/communal balance at play in the culture, a balance (and method of achieving it) inherited from the geographic and social situations of Celtic cultural antecedents. As O'Riordan has noted, the concepts of storytelling and linearity are not necessarily fused in Celtic writing. Stories don't need to follow a chronology to be important or even to *be* stories. What they do instead is follow the teller's thought process.

What I see in Crooks Harper and Kindness, and what I've found myself doing as a writer, is a somewhat stream of consciousness–style of storytelling. It emphasizes the individual nature of the writer's process of judgment and evaluation of their life experiences (and the sometimes impersonal influences shaping these experiences), judgments that are perhaps encouraged in, but not necessarily intended to be forced on, others. Yet it also self-consciously gives credit to the communal forces shaping that individuality. To put it another way, it's like me saying this: my identity and ideas have been shaped by the places, peoples, and stories I've grown up with. However, this book is just my perspective on those things. Saying this is perhaps also a way of protecting those things—if you like what I have to say, I can't take credit: I'm just a reflection of the better people who've come before me. But if you don't like it, well then, it's all on me. Then again, if you don't like what I have to say . . . you're more'n welcome to go write your own book. In fact, please do.

At times the writers seem to write what they're thinking as they think about it, rather than sacrificing thoughts and descriptions they find important to maintain a smoothly chronological narrative that the reader may find more appealing, but altogether less representative of the writer's own experience. I imagine one of the old-fashioned community quilting bees Crooks Harper describes, wherein the materials and work of constructing a quilt were shared. A quilt might be simpler, even more aesthetically pleasing, with fewer and more matching colors; but if I'm not allowed to contribute my length of orange cloth alongside my neighbor's blue, how could it be said that the resulting quilt was really either of ours?

Having and demonstrating our individual judgments seems important both rhetorically and culturally, but this doesn't mean that Appalachian authors have no stake in an audience's reception of their texts. This point allows me to revisit, also, how I am defining these texts as rhetoric, despite their non-conformity with traditionally defined academic rhetorical forms (and, in fact, their sometimes greater correlation with literary forms). "Stream of consciousness" has a storied history in literary fiction and creative nonfiction (having been popularized as a mode of fiction in large part by James Joyce, an Irish writer. Coincidence, do you think?). In what way can I describe these particular narratives, then, as *rhetoric*? I think this is a position wherein Peter Elbow's conception of non-adversarial argument has relevance. As Elbow notes:

> Traditional argument implies a zero-sum game: if I'm right, you must be wrong. Thus, arguments (and essays and dissertations) traditionally start with criticism of the views of opponents. Only in this way—the assumption goes—can I clear any space for my ideas. But this is usually rhetorical suicide with any readers who aren't already on my side. I'm telling them that they can't agree with my ideas unless they first agree that they are wrong or stupid—before they've even heard my allegedly better ideas.[22]

Non-adversarial arguments, in Elbow's view, are rhetorical explorations that look for commonality and assent; in other words, "argu[ing] *for*, not *against*."[23] My position on the narratives that I'm exploring is that they are representative of a regional tradition, but also that they are fundamentally rhetorical rather than creative in purpose, for reasons not at all unlike Elbow's non-adversarial rhetoric. These writers seem, and I'm guessing are, at times writing for themselves, but they also want their readers to take something from their example.

That both Crooks Harper and Kindness expect that the reader will gain *something* from their texts is more than implied. On the back cover of her memoir, Kindness offers her expectation that the stories therein will lead her descendants to "know and be proud of their heritage."[24] For Crooks Harper, the act of writing these stories, an act she refers to as "my time of gathering things together," is so important that it is both "a relief and a pleasure to pass them on to others." These acts of gathering and distributing, the act of writing, is not done without purpose. The writing itself is (perhaps) performed by an individual and demonstrative of "just" that individual's thoughts; however, the role of familial and communal influence on shaping those thoughts is not forgotten. And often, the acknowledgment and binding of those families and communities is part of the purpose. While these Appalachian autobiographies may perhaps be described as a communal effort, in that, as Crooks Harper noted, the stories themselves originate from her, her family, and her place-based community, there is a hesitance to dictate what value the reader should take from that effort, beyond a rather vague *something* of knowledge and pride in what is preserved. In other words, the ideals/values implicit in these discussions, such the preservation of and value for family stories, is understood to be a communal belief; however, the particular interpretations of these stories are also understood to be "only" the writer's own. It is the preservation of the value for place, family, and community, rather than the fleeting individual's perspective on these, that ultimately matters most.

This is a consideration that has much to do with the purposes, if such can be generalized, of Appalachian rhetoric. They are purposes that I, again, tie into ethos. I've gotten the sense that many

Appalachian writers (in which group I include myself) are not necessarily comfortable with the ways academic argumentation asks them to position themselves, as one persuading others of a specific idea or interpretation. However, if persuasion was entirely absent from Appalachian rhetoric as a purpose, what, then, would be our authorial intentions? Let me clarify that I don't think persuasion is absent in these examples; rather, it is non-adversarial. These life narratives are told with a purpose based around preservation and assent, rather than creating change and disconnection. Crooks Harper and Kindness are sharing their process of thinking about place, family, and the social values they attach to these because thinking about these things matters. It is because these things have been thought about, and that process of thinking shared, for generations that I continue to think about them, and value them, today. What we don't do, necessarily, is think about them in the same ways. Neither Kindness nor Crooks Harper seem to insist on any one interpretation of their texts, nor much care whether their readers find their points entertaining or aesthetically pleasing. As I noted, the level of detail can become quite dull to read—although, as each writer is a significant part of her own audience, I doubt she finds these details to be at all dull. But as examples of situated experience, as encouragements to *value* situated experiences, these narratives fulfill a rhetorical purpose in creating, for both the writer and the reader, a world and an ideology to be passed on.

To look at this more specifically: Crooks Harper, in explaining her purpose, again deflects attention from herself per se; she notes that, in the face of "modern hurried living,"[25] it is not her but rather "this location of my birth [that has] many things to offer."[26] But what is interesting is what those offerings are. Crooks Harper is not advocating that we somehow return to outdated methods of living (although she does, like many people, miss the days when doctors made house-calls). As she notes, many of the day-to-day experiences of her own upbringing were based in past contexts that cannot be relived in the present[27]; it makes no sense, for example, to return to horse-drawn wagons as a primary mode of transportation, although she does describe in detail what role horses played in the maintenance of her family and farm. Instead, what her narratives, her composed life experiences, can demonstrate is a way of maintaining communal bonds in times of change, "even though it is not always by choice that we face [these changes]."[28] In other words, while the details of life may change, particularly from generation to generation, the values for place and community need not. While most of us no longer rely on rain barrels for our water (though, given the influence climate change is having on rain patterns, this is perhaps an old-fashioned device that more of us ought to revisit), Crooks Harper nonetheless explains the importance of the rain barrel for supplying water in her childhood. She "mourns the passing of the rain barrel"[29] not because she dislikes having running water today, but because she sees importance in what the rain barrel represented for her: sustenance, self-sufficiency, and curiosity about the world around her. She explains that as a child the rain barrel "raised questions in my young mind. How did that frog get into the barrel? How could he breathe in that deep, dark chasm? What would he do when the barrel got empty?"[30] The point, as I read it, is that Crooks Harper is writing to create and preserve ideas and knowledges that have potential social value; not just how to use a rain barrel, but what having a rain barrel says about her upbringing and the desire to live well in the place that fostered that upbringing. What her writing says to me, in a wider sense, is that it is important to be self-sufficient, to understand the environment, to find ways to sustain.

What she does not say is that her upbringing is better than others, or that the lifeways of herself, her family, and her neighbors ought to be adopted by all. Rather, Crooks Harper says to us, as I interpret her, *I've created my quilt, a vision of my world built by my words. It is a vision I value, and I invite you to share.* It is something both individual, in that the vision itself is very much reflective of her own thoughts and interpretations, but also communal; this invitation to her audience to both assent and to build their own visions is one that Crooks Harper expects at least some of her readers to take up.

My sense, then, is that both Crooks Harper and Kindness are deflecting attention from themselves as authors (not a move that I perceive as conventional in more mainstream memoir) in service of a rhetorical purpose: they are working to preserve, through language and communal assent, something much larger than themselves, a lifestyle based on recognized (for their audience) ideals of community social values revolving around place and family. Specifically, what I'm seeing in the rhetoric is a reliance on place and family not only as socially important concepts (which they are), but also an implicit understanding that these are sources of knowledge on which to build one's process of thinking and identity-building. In other words, the concepts of "place" and "family" can be defined much more widely in this form of Appalachian rhetoric, a width that pushes these concepts beyond the bounds of abstraction and into something tangled up with threads of self-definition. Place, in these texts, can be family, and family can be place. And the stories that we tell of each are no less part of us because they were sometimes first told to us by our mothers and grandmothers; they shape us as much as the stories we create ourselves.

To provide a perhaps useful overview of my thinking at this point: what I'm seeing in the texts, as examples of a written Appalachian rhetoric, is a focus on individual perspective, in that the writers are essentially creating and demonstrating their construction of social values for place and family/community. They emphasize humility in this individualism (in that these are, as they carefully note, *only their* perspectives, which they do not insist be shared by all), a humility that encourages connection and assent over dissension. However, they as authors are not exceptional, aren't telling us what to think. Rather, they're sharing with the reader their process of thinking and valuing aspects of their lives. Likewise, they take steps to emphasize that the idea of "individual" can and does include other peoples, even places; in other words, while these texts are individual perspectives, they give credit to other forces in shaping their perspectives. The narratives are complicated, in that they defy strict chronological organization or focus on specific events, yet by doing so they demonstrate a fuller picture of each author's thought process while composing, a thought process that occasionally slips the reins of clear organization and transitioning.

I can't help thinking again, here, of my great-grandmother's quilts. Why exactly did she place a red and orange paisley within an almost neon green? I have no idea . . . but I trust that it made sense to her. As Amy Clark explained in her article "Letters from Home: The Literate Lives of Central Appalachian Women," quilters chose design and materials with purpose, sometimes artistic but also "to preserve family history and to keep the art alive."[31] In my own quilt, I can choose different colors and different patterns; assuming, of course, that I've understood that quilting is something worth doing.

Where I see these texts as being particularly rhetorical, and where I see the Celtic rhetorical tradition coming into focus, is in what I read as the purpose of these texts: the demonstration of a process of judgment, about the means by which the things we value shape our lives, and how we'd like to see them shape lives in the future. Like the *Acallam*, these texts are linguistically tying the authors, and perhaps their readers, to places and communities. While I see these as written rhetorical acts, aiming to persuade the reader to accept particular social values and ways of thinking, they are not forthright or forceful in that persuasion; rather they hedge, they hint, they encourage and invite without attempting to overtly insist.

———

Of course, this is just the evidence of two texts, and the readings of them are just my own interpretations. Yet I don't think that makes them invalid; the ways Crooks Harper and Kindness are writing their stories are the ways I'd write (am writing) mine, too. With the ever-present understanding that readers may take what they will from anything I do write, and that those interpretations may differ from my own, I will hazard to say what I take from my process of thinking: that Appalachian rhetoric can be and has been written, and at least some aspects of it have a history that influences both what gets written and how. Clark has emphasized that for Appalachian educators and students, we need to realize that "home literacies and academic literacies *can* exist harmoniously"[32]; Crooks Harper and Kindness demonstrate for me what that merging might look like in writing. They prove that Appalachian authors can tell their stories in writing without sacrificing how those stories are told. But I'll hazard even further to say that I think understanding this history, for those of us influenced by it, can play an important role in how others think of us and how we think of ourselves. To start, it can demonstrate that differences in the writing classroom aren't always about mistakes or ignorance; they can be about cultural rhetoric.

Todd Snyder said something at a recent guest lecture that sticks with me. He said that he likes stories that don't always end up where you think they will, but that this is an impulse he has to curb when composing a text for mainstream academic publishers. Like Todd, I don't think we always know, in starting our stories, where exactly we'll end up; and if you're an Appalachian writer, maybe that's just fine. That is part of the telling, the journey, the process of building for ourselves the world through our thinking, our judgment, and letting others listen in. I've taken some turns I didn't foresee at the start, or maybe I've quilted in some cloths that didn't quite match but that, for me, fit the pattern I'm following. It's a pattern of loops and webs perhaps, but it's a web that keeps bringing me back around in my head to those Scotch-Irish, planting homesteads up and down Appalachia three hundred years ago.

I'm not trying to say that all Appalachian texts are identical to some historical precedent, or even that Scotch-Irish rhetorical influence is the only force shaping how we think, act, speak, and write. There are, as has been noted, many more cultural influences on Appalachia than are often credited or acknowledged; nor can we simply say that Appalachian rhetoric merely replicates past forms in unchanged ways, without reference to modern life and modern exigencies. Any form of culture that didn't adapt with changing needs and situations would surely die out. What I'm examining is one of the influences our rhetoric may have adapted *from*. In fact, Scotch-Irish linguistic and rhetorical history has traditionally been open to adaptation. While my focus has not necessarily been on vocabulary, in terms of spoken or written dialect choices, it is still significant to me that the Scotch-Irish vocabulary brought to Appalachia has been remarkably adaptable. Michael Montgomery argues that while the underlying grammar of Appalachian dialect remains that of the Scotch-Irish, the vocabulary is a different story. Also, Gary Carden, in the documentary *Mountain Talk,* attributes the formation of newer vocabulary to "the Scots-Irish talent for improvisation." Maybe what I'm seeing in these texts is to my rhetoric what the Scotch-Irish grammar still is to aspects of my home language: part of a deep structure, a part that holds on while the details get improvised.

I also don't wish to indicate that all Appalachian people will write or communicate in ways identical to each other, or to create a measurement by which to define Appalachian-ness in a text or a person. Not all Appalachian peoples have identical experiences, for a variety of reasons. For example, as I've noted before, many Appalachian people grow up in coal towns or Rust Belt industrial centers; I did not, nor did the authors I've examined. It's also worth noting that not all Appalachians today live in Appalachia, a state that promises fruitful future questions: how does one account for the role place plays in personal or family identity, when the place in which one lives has changed?

So what am I trying to say with this? What does it matter if Appalachian rhetoric and culture are influenced by a Celtic tradition? For one thing, it could simply provide explanation for why some of us feel influenced to communicate in particular ways; when Geneva Smitherman taught me that AAVE grew from roots in African languages and ways of speaking, my worldview opened up wider than it had been before. And as someone who does value heritage, for either individual or cultural reasons, I wholeheartedly admit to wanting Appalachia to have a rhetorical history, something I can hold up like a shield when told that I simply talk or write *wrong*. I'm trying, ultimately, to raise possibilities that have gone unseen: that there may be different influences prompting Appalachian writers in the classroom, influences related to a cultural heritage, and which are not simply attributable to having never learned the academically correct ways of writing. If our rhetoric is a link with an alternative rhetorical tradition (that of the Celts), and if that rhetoric continues to serve my community, then that fact says something about us, about what we value and how we live with each other and with the land. As Lynch noted, the typically rural, decentralized lifestyle of Celtic people required an alternate rhetoric to that proposed by the urban Greeks and Romans.[33] I can't help but recall this point when I read the section of her memoir when Kindness describes a spread-out Appalachian community in which farms touched, but houses didn't. It makes sense to me that a style of rhetoric adapted to fit a similar geography a world away can fit in the region of my birth, too.

Of course, demonstrating that this form of Appalachian rhetoric has a cultural history does not matter to everyone's view. After we read letters to the editor about fracking in my environmental rhetoric class, I tried explaining to the students my sense of the rhetoric we were seeing in them. I told the class about the Celtic rhetorical history I was studying and how that heritage could influence communication and values. One of my non-Appalachian students snorted, "If you can see how your culture hasn't changed since the Dark Ages, well, that's not exactly something to be proud of, is it?"

I wanted to say, Appalachia just can't win with people like you, can it? When mainstream rhetoric demonstrates its precedents in Greco-Roman rhetoric, it comes across as "classical"; when we reach through time for our own intellectual precedents, we're accused of living in the Dark Ages. I thought this, but again, I didn't say it. To paraphrase Marilou Awiakta, generations of Appalachian ancestors kept me from being that confrontational, at least with someone who was, essentially, a stranger. Angers, once kindled, aren't always easy to put out. Instead, I said, speaking only for myself, "Well, I'm proud of it." Those ancestors also taught me, it seems, that *confrontational* and *contrary* aren't necessarily the same thing.

Of course, there's a lot going on in this student's response. It's an indication of how little we know Celtic history in this country: the "Dark Ages" for most of Europe was actually a time in which the Celtic Fringe enjoyed the best educational system and most humane social policies on the continent. But also, he pretty well articulated the risks inherent in any connection of modern Appalachia with the past. The result can be an easy assumption not only of our backwardness, but that it is a backwardness we have chosen. We thus must be held liable to the repercussions, which can be anything from poor schools, poverty, pollution, and lack of decent healthcare. (When one chooses to live in the Dark Ages, what does one expect?) Of course, too much interest in the past also clashes with mainstream America's fetish for newness. In a society that seems often to privilege change, even for the worse, over sustainability or preservation, Appalachia is out of the gate deemed unsuitable, ignorant . . . nothing to be proud of.

Except, as I said, I am proud of it. Sometimes it takes more strength and creativity to knit things together than to rip them apart, and like the man in Stephen Fry's documentary, who cannot play his music without feeling the threads connecting him to history and the land itself, I cannot look at my rhetoric without seeing the same. I want Nathan Shepley's student Matt, and his other teachers, to know that there is perhaps a reason why writing in certain ways and about certain things feels right. And while I'm hesitant to tell Matt how he should feel about this reason, this heritage, I can say that I know how I feel about it. And Matt, if you're reading this, you're welcome to feel the same way, too.

CHAPTER 6

When Rhetoric Is a Deficit

While my work thus far has primarily focused on the historical roots of an Appalachian rhetorical tradition, I also want to consider how that tradition has been received in our current educational system. Long story short, it largely hasn't been received there at all. "School" predominantly remains a place for learning and practicing standardized forms of language, writing, and rhetoric. While I don't dispute the importance of knowing multiple styles of communication, particularly when learning these allows for personal growth and development, my concern is that standard written English isn't presented as one option in most Appalachian schools; rather, it's presented as the only correct way. This narrowing becomes a problem when we consider what the field of rhetoric and composition has long argued: that discourse is about more than words, it's about what James Paul Gee calls an "identity kit"[1] that can influence thought, action, and self-esteem. What happens when Appalachian students get the message that their home discourses, and by extension identities, are bad? They learn that Appalachia is bad, too.

In this chapter, I want to look more closely at why comparatively few schools are making Appalachian rhetoric and identity part of students' classroom experience. Like most everything involving Appalachia, I think the reasons are more complicated then they get credit for: they spill the banks of educational theory alone and overflow into wider societal ideas about success, economic class, and what it means to be "Appalachian" at all.

———

One of the nearest towns to where my family lives ("town" being a term I'm not sure many would bother to apply, it being that small) has a festival every summer that we used to call "the Homecoming." While I'm not certain about the origin of this name, it seems likely to me that it meant exactly what it implied: this was to be a time of homecoming for those perhaps far-flung former residents, many who likely left when the railroad stopped running and took the town's prosperity with it. So each year a couple hundred people descend on this little place to chat, eat fried pies and steak sandwiches, watch their kids march or ride their horses in a parade, and view the fireworks display that is put on now rather than on the 4th of July, in the festival's honor.

When I was about five or six years old, the festival's name officially changed to "The Folk Festival." I remember asking Pap, "Why'd they change it? I like the name 'Homecoming.'" Pap replied, "Well, this'n works too. It's a folk festival, and we're hill folk." This exchange stuck with me because it was the first time I ever heard that there was a name for what we were, or that we even were *something*. And in retrospect, I think it's important to note that the name my grandfather applied to us was based on place, on the geographic location of "the hills," and the term "folk," which has associations with ruralness. *But no part of that self-descriptive term had anything to do with poverty.*

Something I've heard more than once, from people inside and outside of Appalachia, is "When I was a kid, I never knew we were poor." For example, Katherine Kelleher Sohn cites an Appalachian informant in Virginia Seitz's study, who recalls, "I didn't know I was poor white trash until I went to school and somebody told me. If I had never gone to school, I never would have known I was poor."[2] This was somewhat true for me, too; in retrospect it's clearer than it felt at the time. We lived in a trailer. For a long time, we all slept in one room; the living room, with its wood-burning stove, was the only room with real heat in the winter. My mom told me once that for a phase of about eight years during my childhood, she hardly ever had new clothes; any money she got went toward providing for her kids. When I was little, my father worked as a day laborer for a road construction company. He had started this work soon out of high school; he was laid off most winters, when there was no work. But he was good at his job. Mom told me once that Dad could look at a job site and just know what needed done. He worked his way up to steadier and more lucrative administrative jobs. His skills made him sought after by several companies, both in the US and outside it. His last employer was based out of London, England. (There were some highly comic exchanges between my father, whose language choices taught me the major curse words while most kids were learning their ABCs, and these very proper English businessmen that are told like legends in the family even today.) By the time he retired, my father was a well-paid construction company supervisor, and we had built and moved into a new house where everyone had a separate bedroom, something that took me years to get used to.

But here's the thing. Once, before he retired, the company my father worked for set out to hire for the position directly below his, one he had moved up from several years earlier. Come to find out that now, among the absolutely mandatory job requirements, was a college degree. My father, were he to start out today and attempt to recreate his career path, with the exact same work ethic, experience, knowledge, and skill he applied before, would simply be unable to rise above that day laborer position. The system, not my father, has changed too much for that. I can't help but wonder what, on the basis of this new rule, the company thought about my dad's ability at his work, given that he lacked the degree they now believed was essential. Did they think he was just lucky? That he was some kind of savant? I wonder, too, if he had taken the route now expected—a degree leading directly into a management position—if he would have been as good as he was. I of all people don't want to argue against the value of a college education (which, for the record, I think has great value, and I don't just mean economically). But I also know that my dad never had any desire to go to college. He wanted to earn a living, to work. Because he did, my parents could afford to send me to college; because he believed that physical work, not education, was his path in life, I was able to make education mine. But the opportunity to make that choice is disappearing for the many Appalachians who continue to feel more at home with the idea of work than school. Why do these paths seem so distinct for so many of us? I have concerns not only about the separation of work and education as concepts (and, by extension, the message that work in particular is more right for us), but also that the culture around us promotes this distinction.

———

My ancestors worked. There has always been, of course, that full-time, unpaid domestic work that is required to keep body and soul together for oneself and one's children. But what I mean, too, is that they did economic work as well. My great-great-grandparents farmed. My grandmother's father worked in a stone quarry; Great-Grandma Carpenter always remembered the pain she felt at seeing him off to work, in January, to hew rock with no gloves. My grandfather's family farmed and mined coal; they didn't work for a coal company, which is, in retrospect, a relief, but rather they dug from the hillsides and sold by the bucket to their neighbors. (As it has been described to me: "Father dug, Mother hauled, Kids sorted.") When Pap came back from WWII, minus an arm and an eye, he had fewer options for physical labor. Instead, he learned television repair and opened a shop in an old coal shack he had hauled back to the house. Much of his work saw him traveling the countryside to repair TVs, back in the day when electronics were actually repaired rather than replaced.

There are inequalities implicit in this list, not least of which is the fact that nearly all economically remunerative jobs were, in those times, the provinces of men. I'm not implying that the women didn't work perhaps much harder than their male partners, only that they often did so without direct pay. But I also notice that many of the jobs in my direct heritage—quarryman, miner, construction laborer—are ultimately physical forms of work. They weren't people who were expected to make a living by what they thought, and they were educated accordingly.

Todd Snyder's book *The Rhetoric of Appalachian Identity* explores the complicated dynamics of Appalachian "work." Using a Marxist lens, Snyder explains that ideologies of manual labor, often underpaid and unsafe, become entwined with ideologies of masculinity.[3] The result is a sense of defensiveness toward the very processes that keep such workers dis-empowered. So, Appalachia becomes part of a cyclical system of multigenerational (often male) manual laborers with little access to material or educational advantages, influenced both without and within to see the system as normal, even laudable. Real men do real (physical) work.

Having been ingrained in the system Snyder describes, my immediate reaction to these stories of ancestral work is pride. I'm proud of "Grandpa Jake," working a pick-ax bare-handed in the winter cold to buy warm boots for his kids. But it is a pride, as Snyder has shown, that is problematic: I wonder now, did Grandpa Jake feel like this was his lot in life, his "man's work," something to take pride in despite its small rewards? Why did Grandpa Jake have to work so hard, for so little? And more than that, why couldn't he have been a schoolteacher, a doctor, a college professor—in other words, a job where his thoughts mattered as much as his muscles? *Why didn't the world care what he thought? Why do they still not?*

There seems to be an ideology at play here, inside and outside the region, that says Appalachian peoples, particularly but not exclusively men, are for work—physical, blue-collar work. Education isn't real work, and it isn't really something meant for them. This feeling can deeply influence people's lives and choices. Mick Mulvaney, the director of the White House Office of Budget and Management, said on March 16, 2017, that it was unfair for coal miners to pay taxes to support PBS.[4] Among the implications here is, of course, that something as education-focused as PBS has no real relevance for a coal miner. They aren't thinkers, they are workers. There's a difference. It isn't fair that they should have to support the people who are thinkers. Also, this statement implies that providing education through things like PBS *to* coal miners is a waste. Again, these people don't think. They don't need educational resources.

I don't intend to dwell here on the gender politics or social implications of work necessarily (Snyder has done valuable research on this subject), but I do want to consider how work as the route to economic success is more complicated than is conveyed by the dominant story we're sold in Appalachia. Because if nothing else, I hope my above stated "work genealogy" shows one thing: I don't come from a lazy people. But we are, broadly speaking, also not a rich people. And that seems, from my perspective, to be the sticking point in so much of how we are viewed and defined. However, education as a route to success is also not a straightforward story because what we learn, how we learn, and if we learn at all can be deeply influenced by cultural stereotypes and expectations. These dynamics can all have implications regarding voice and who gets heard.

What is that American dream, again? Oh yes: work hard, and you'll succeed ("success," of course, bringing certain monetary rewards). If we work, yet do not "succeed" in gaining the economic outcome the narrative says we should—if we work and yet stay poor—there must be something wrong with us. Right? Maybe the problem is, then, not that we don't work, but that we just aren't educated enough for success. But what about those of us who get the message early on that school isn't something relevant for us, isn't part of our identity?

Historian Ron Eller and social justice advocate Helen Lewis have both placed the blame for Appalachian economic inequality not on the people themselves but largely on corporations in the extraction industry that mask exploitation under the label of "progress."[5] But why do so many seem so willing to believe that economic and social inequality is ultimately our fault? I worry that we, inside and outside the region, are at least tacitly being educated to believe that it is.

———

I want to return here to the Banned Terms Project I discussed earlier. The project, entailing a joint effort by the college's English and communications departments to standardize regional features of students' language, was the result of a deeply influential faculty meeting. This meeting featured a guest speaker, representing Ruby Payne's educational consultation organization, aha! Process, Inc. Payne's influence stems from her 1996 book *A Framework for Understanding Poverty*, a text that outlines the concepts about which she has continued to write and speak, to tremendous popularity. Payne advocates educating teachers and others (including law enforcement and political officials[6]) about the "culture" of poverty. Specifically, she argues that each social class (poverty class, middle class, and upper class) operates on its own distinguishable rules. Impoverished people remain impoverished because they don't know the "rules" of the middle class, rules that dictate language, behavior, and social values. For example, Payne explains that among the rules of poverty is that "any extra money is shared

. . . people are possessions . . . the mother is the most powerful figure . . . food is equated with love . . . [and] separation is not an option."[7] The poverty mindset is one that is both criminal and violent; "the line between what is legal and illegal is thin and often crossed . . . . The poor simply see jail as a part of life and not necessarily always bad."[8] This is just a selection of poverty's "hidden rules," all of which are presented as negative, the adherence to which keeps people trapped in cycles of generational poverty. Payne argues that teachers can be, for poor students, perhaps their only "appropriate role model[s],"[9] who educate them in the rules of middle-class thought and behavior. Payne's characterizations of "poverty culture" cross other cultural or ethnic boundaries. Throughout her book, Payne creates hypothetical situations to illustrate her points, "scenarios" based around interchangeably white, African American, and Hispanic characters who demonstrate the values and mindsets Payne ascribes to poverty culture. Yet, while poverty is the disease, school can be the cure. Schools bear the responsibility, she argues, for fixing "students who bring the poverty culture with them [and who are] increasing in numbers,"[10] by essentially teaching students to adhere to a standardized, middle-class culture.

The rules of middle-class thought and behavior that Payne wants to see taught are deeply entwined with conceptions of rhetoric. Payne separates discourse into a "formal" (middle-class) and "informal" (poverty-class) register; however, she describes the formal register as definable by the characteristics of "sequence, order, cause and effect, and a conclusion: all skills necessary for problem-solving [and] inference."[11] The informal register, on the other hand, is merely more entertaining. In essence, Payne argues that standardized academic modes of communication, modes she describes as the realm of the middle class, are alone capable of producing the cognitive effects of problem-solving and inference. Meanwhile the informal dialects of the poverty class (which by their nature lack "sequence, order, cause and effect, and a conclusion") very literally produce ignorance in the minds of their users. The inference becomes that you can't use the poverty-class, informal register and still be a skilled, sophisticated thinker.

Julie Keown-Bomar and Deborah Pattee have noted the effect these ideologies have had on educators:

> Many participants fresh out of a Payne workshop are impressed, leaving motivated with the belief that they can help students learn skills they need in order to assimilate to a middle class culture and, therefore, move out of poverty. Some feel they had more cross-class compassion, an enlightened understanding of people different from themselves, and an increased desire to help.[12]

Is it any surprise that the faculty at my former Appalachian community college came away from this meeting with a renewed desire to get rid of the regional dialect? It turned out that what was "wrong" with us, what kept us in poverty, was something very simple, with a very simple solution: standardize the language, and you will standardize the people—and their income. Of course the problem is that it's not so simple at all.

———

Roberta Ahlquist, Paul C. Gorski, and Theresa Montano have problematized Payne's ideology; as they argue, "Payne has made her millions and grown her empire by selling a theoretical framework, the 'culture of poverty,' which, for all intents and purposes, was dispelled, empirically and philosophically, as mythology by the early 1970s."[13] Poverty-culture theory is based fundamentally on deficit ideology, "which locates societal problems as existing *within* rather than as pressing *upon* disenfranchised communities."[14] Yet as a theory, and as a set of practices prompted by that theory, Payne's culture of poverty ideology continues to thrive. As Ahlquist, Gorski, and Montano note, "district after district pay her tens of thousands of dollars or more to misinform them."[15] Gorski in particular raises the concern that what this ideology does is to mistake difference for deficit in a way that prevents us from recognizing and resisting domination.[16] Poverty is reified as a state created by individual choice, as a reflection of the moral and mental weakness ingrained by poverty culture,[17] while teachers are encouraged to focus on "'fixing' disenfranchised communities rather than the policies and practices which disenfranchise them."[18]

I don't mean to single Payne out as the "problem" that prevents the kind of productive role I'd like to see for Appalachia in classrooms and wider society. What Payne advocates is hardly new or limited to only her; E. D. Hirsch, for example, has also long been a vocal and respected educational voice urging greater curricular standardization as a means of achieving social equality. And, in fact, Payne does not specify Appalachia by name in any of her poverty culture "scenarios"; part of her project is to unite all poverty into one culture, regardless of racial or geographic factors.[19] Rather, she is a highly visible example of the kinds of thinking—specifically, the deficit ideology and economic perceptions fueling it—that influence how Appalachian peoples can be problematically perceived, defined, and treated in educational arenas.

However, despite the absence of the term "Appalachia" in her work, Payne's arguments and those like them have very real effects for Appalachia. I've witnessed it. As I said, it was a guest lecture by one of Ruby Payne's aha! Process, Inc. associates that resulted in my former college's Banned Terms Project. The case was made exceptionally clear: the problems "keeping our students poor" were not effects of exploitative industrial practices and prejudicial policies; they were the discourses our students chose to use and the identities and mindsets that prompted those choices. By very

specifically connecting discourse with violence and shallow thinking, Payne articulated a time-honored association between language and morality/intelligence. Our students' poverty mindset
creates and is reflected by their incorrect English, ways of organiz-
ing thoughts, and ways of conveying information. In this ideology,
language is a problem that can and should be changed by dedicated
teachers. In fact, this philosophy promises to do what so many
teachers long to do: make students' lives better. Who, after all,
wants to be poor, to feel trapped and helpless to better provide for
themselves and their families? What isn't asked, however, is not
"who wants to be poor?" but rather "who wants to be Appalachian?"
By arguing that all impoverished peoples share ingrained traits,
including social values, language values, and rhetorical practices,
Payne effectively erases any other forms of cultural distinctiveness,
never mind viewing these as worthy of celebration. What
Appalachian students have to offer academic ideals of multiculturalism becomes even less visible. And I would argue that some of us
do want to be Appalachian, or would, if "Appalachian" and "poor"
weren't defined as one and the same. Especially since both designa-
tions have come to represent the same thing in the Payne-style ideology: violence, stupidity, and lack of self-respect.

Poverty culture is not a new concept, having been popularized
in the 1960s by anthropologist Oscar Lewis. However, what I see
Payne bringing to the debate is an increasingly intentional erasure
of cultural difference within this model. Payne's lumped definition
of poverty culture not only allows for an easier correlation of
"Appalachia" with, at root, "poverty." It also allows for a leveling
effect that other scholars have noticed, in which ideas about or
artifacts of Appalachian culture, including stereotypes, are being
applied to all impoverished or even simply rural areas. For example, Kim Donehower notes that all rurality is increasingly painted
as essentially, and stereotypically, Appalachian. She describes the
2002 annual meeting of the Rural Sites Network of the National

Writing Project, where participants were asked to wear bandanas, listen to bluegrass music, and participate in an opening cheer of "yee-hah,"[20] even though most of the participants were from non-Appalachian rural areas in the American West.[21] Likewise, Todd Snyder was surprised at the response his discussions of Appalachian identity got from students in New York: "they seemed somewhat unwilling to grant Appalachian culture status as a recognizable and authentic culture," preferring instead to argue that what Snyder identified as issues directly related to Appalachian experiences were not culturally related. According to one student, "The obstacles [Snyder] faced aren't that different from the problems of a first-generation college student from small-town Maine or Vermont."[22] It's interesting to me that this student chose Maine and Vermont as comparatives, as the Appalachian Mountain chain does extend through New England in addition to the more recognized mountains in the South, but I doubt that's what this student was thinking. Instead, he seems to have been thinking that all poverty produces the same effects; as primarily products of poverty culture, all cultures of Appalachia are no different than any other place where people are poor.

These definitions concern me deeply. Appalachia has long been defined in wider American society not by culture but by economic class (or the effects of poverty). As previously noted, the Appalachian Regional Commission considers poverty as inextricable from their existential purpose and the very definition of what Appalachia is. Even my alma mater, Ohio University, which is the only major research university in Appalachian Ohio, makes the same correlation. The report "Appalachian Perspectives at Ohio University: Findings of Spring 2004 Survey" introduces the university's regional surroundings with a definition focusing on multigenerational poverty. I'm not arguing against the truthfulness or even usefulness of discussing Appalachian poverty. What concerns me is that this discussion over-relies on one characteristic to define

Appalachian identity, to the point of obscuring, particularly for non-regional audiences, other potential factors in the ways that the people might view themselves. In fact, the second part of this report offers an interesting counterpoint: when the actual participants in the surveys identified themselves as Appalachian, they did so "largely based upon (a) ties to family and place, (b) heritage and traditions, and (c) personal values"[23] . . . not based on shared poverty.

What specifically troubles me is that defining Appalachia primarily, at times it seems even solely, in terms of economic poverty risks denying the very differences in cultural origins and influences that make rhetorical styles unique. Kim Donehower has described the ways Appalachian origin and identity have been (wrongly) identified as inherently, and persistently, Anglo-Saxon. It is a conflation in which Celtic influence, let alone influence from other cultures, nationalities, and ethnic groups, is either ignored or lumped together with a sort of vague European whiteness. And it is this last point that may be the most significant factor in the conflation. When Appalachia is painted as "representative of whiteness, of 'pure' Anglo-Saxon culture, protected from racial or ethnic contamination by being shut away in the mountains," Appalachian people become defined as "the 'contemporary ancestors' of modern [American] civilization,"[24] who through our own perverseness have simply failed to advance. Donehower considers the reasoning behind this conflation as one of regional scapegoating—it emphasizes the superiority of non-Appalachian, mainstream white America, who, through nothing but choice and action, have become "intellectually, culturally, economically, and morally" better than us. By extension, we, having (according to the myth) started identically, bear the culpability of choices that result in negative repercussions, socially, educationally, and economically. This makes compassionate people, as educators often are, see Appalachia as a "problem to be solved."[25] We can, in other words, be "caught up," a process that entails, in ideologies such as Ruby

Payne's, teaching us to want the values of our middle-class, mainstream, white kinfolk.

———

Last summer an oil man came to see my father. His company was proposing a pipeline project, and he wanted permission for it to cross our farm. At one point, my brother asked him what risks this project had for the underlying water table. The oil man, who'd been basically polite up till this point, shook his head. "What is it with you people?" he asked. "We're offering to make you rich, and all you want to know about is the water. *Just move away.*"

Believe it or not, I was delighted by this exchange. It was a thrill to see an honest opinion from an industry rep, for one thing. But he also clarified a few things for me that I appreciated: more than just my family were worried about our water and more than just us were refusing to abandon ancestral lands to Big Oil. So many so, apparently, that an exasperated oil rep referred to us as *you people.* If we were culturally the same as he was, wouldn't most all of us have valued the same things? Wouldn't we have done what he accepted as common sense: thanked him for his "offer," grabbed our cash, and run? What I've seen happening in reality is something far more complicated: plenty have taken the cash for oil and pipeline leases, it's true. But I don't know a one of them that's moved away.

We could talk about this as something problematic, as it certainly can be. Todd Snyder has critiqued the concept of "holme"[26] in Appalachian culture; too great a reliance on place to ground identity can be damaging to opportunity or even health, if one refuses to leave lands polluted by industrial waste and pollution. Yet, Appalachian identity need not be solely based in geography. As he pointed out in a recent guest lecture, "I'll be Appalachian, no matter where I live," a statement that in itself indicates there is something ideological to Appalachian identity, a presence rather than a deficit of culture. But what is most important for me, at this point, is simply considering the possibility of seeing these dynamics as *cultural* at all and not simply formed through poverty, through shared need. Maybe we take the money, but at least some of us want the water and the land, too. Surely if all we were was a united collective of poverty, the money would be enough.

———

I tried teaching a junior-level writing and rhetoric class at my former university that focused largely on rhetorical constructions of Appalachia. In the class we read texts and watched films about Appalachia, some produced by and some not produced by Appalachians. I based the overall approach for the course on the tenets of place-based pedagogy; as scholar and teacher Paula Mathieu explains, "We believe that mindfulness about places—critical thinking, close observation, and personal reflection—can help us better understand ourselves and our environment while we also hone the very skills necessary for academic success."[27] Only one student in this class was local and identified herself as Appalachian, but I figured that no matter what their origins, they lived here now. Wherever they landed in the future, they would live not only with people, but also in places, and I hoped they could begin to learn to live in those places well, thoughtfully, and sustainably.

However, no matter how I described the exigency or value of this approach, the course ended up being a hard, and largely unsuccessful, sell. I remember one student's anonymous course evaluation response saying that the study of Appalachian rhetoric was ultimately pointless. As he or she put it, "a lot of this class was about Appalachia. Seriously, who cares?" Appalachia is something removed, something unimportant, even for the outsiders who choose to live there. (If it is, after all, fundamentally a deficit culture, who in their right mind would want to deeply contemplate Appalachia?) This dismissive attitude is one I've since come to feel is tied to the "official" story of what Appalachia is: it is a place, and by extension people, defined by the mutating effects of poverty. A ten-week term simply could not shake that belief.

However, not all students shared the opinion that they need not care about Appalachia. The "deficit" culture definition awakens for some an alternate attitude, one that says people should care, but in a way I find almost as concerning. It's an attitude shaped by compassion rather than contempt: mainstream America must "help" Appalachian peoples be better. The way this attitude came into play in my class was articulated by one student, Lisa, who earnestly explained that students could do much more to help the Appalachian people in the local region. She was speaking, specifically, along the lines of charity work, encouraging her classmates to donate their old clothes to organizations such as Goodwill. "We need to help these people!" she said. I didn't want to criticize this attitude, and I was delighted that she recognized and disliked the level of disconnection between the university and the surrounding region. But I couldn't help feeling uncomfortable, too—it seemed like a different shade of the same story: we hill folk are either pointless or we need help, but either way, both attitudes position us as having nothing to offer. While Lisa was speaking, I wondered what Ella, my one Appalachian student, was thinking. I pondered the ethical implications of asking her directly. Turns out, I didn't have to; she volunteered her thoughts. Ella raised her hand and, turning to Lisa, said, "I appreciate what you're saying, and I don't mean to sound rude, but . . . I can't think of anybody who'd say they *want* your help."

———

Sharyn McCrumb recounts an incident in North Carolina during a particularly bad winter in 1960. She says it illustrates a central factor of the Celtic-influenced Appalachian character:

> Two Red Cross workers had heard about an old woman in her eighties who lived in a cabin way back in the hills, and they volunteered to take a jeep to bring help to her. The two volunteers drove up the ice-bound road as far as they could, abandoned the jeep when the road became impassable, got out snow shoes, wrestled them on, and helped each other tramp through the waist-deep snow until, finally, they saw the little curl of chimney smoke up on the ridge that told them they'd found her. They managed to hike to the cabin on the top of the hill, stomped up on the porch, and rapped on the door. Finally the old lady opened it. The rescuers announced proudly, "We're from the Red Cross." "Oh honey," she replied. "It has been such a hard winter, I don't think I can help you this year."[28]

I see potential rhetorical repercussion in the image this story gives of Appalachian character—meaning, I'm concerned that the response to that character could easily be, "Why should we care if there's decent medical care, working conditions, and educational opportunities in Appalachia? Why should we care if industries run roughshod over the land and people there? They obviously don't want 'help.'" But I also think it's noteworthy that in this story, there is nothing about the woman personally that indicates that she *needs*, certainly not in the way that we have been rhetorically defined from the outside as being nothing but need . . . as a problem to be either solved or ignored.

I occasionally watch cartoons. Honestly, they're sometimes the best storylines available on television. One of my recent favorites was *Avatar: The Last Airbender*. There was one episode in which the character Iro (the wise and patient uncle of troubled, xenophobic teenager Zuko) tries to explain to his nephew the benefits of a multicultural outlook, using the four "nations" existing in the show's mythology:

> Fire is the element of power. The people of the Fire Nation have desire and will, and the energy and drive to achieve what they want. Earth is the element of substance. The people of the Earth Kingdom are diverse and strong; they are persistent and enduring. Air is the element of freedom. The Air Nomads detached themselves from worldly concerns, and found peace and freedom. (Also, they apparently had pretty good senses of humor!) Water is the element of change. The people of the Water Tribe are capable of adapting to many things. They have a deep sense of community and love that holds them together through anything. . . . It is important to draw wisdom from many different places. If you take it from only one place, it becomes rigid and stale.[29]

I know, intellectually, that boiling anything like a real, living culture into any one sentence is impossible to do with accuracy or fairness. And I also know that looking at multiculturalism solely from the perspective of what one can gain from it is somewhat selfish. Yet still, when I watched this episode, I had to rewind and listen again. *"It is important to draw wisdom from many different places. If you take it from only one place, it becomes rigid and stale."* I don't remember any of the cartoons from my childhood articulating so clearly the ideal of multiculturalism, let alone the way cultural diversity can keep knowledge itself vital, alive. Wouldn't it be nice if the kids who grow up having heard this message also grow up thinking of Appalachia as part of that multicultural fabric? What if Appalachia was seen and accepted as one of the places from which to draw wisdom, a region that could nourish our nation's, our world's, intellect?

I don't think that is something we do see, though. Appalachia is, instead, the negative image of intellectual achievement, the inverse of wisdom and education. I find myself thinking again of the opening pages of Katherine Kelleher Sohn's groundbreaking text, *Whistlin' and Crowin' Women of Appalachia: Literacy Practices since College*, where Sohn recalled witnessing professors at a CCCC in Nashville, Tennessee, mocking their Appalachian waiter's accent.[30] Cultures have their own forms of wisdom, of knowledge, that academia at large, at least in my experience of it, says are worthy of respect. Yet too often, Appalachia simply does not seem to qualify.

I am concerned by what Appalachian cultural erasure can mean for us and our ideas about self-identity and educational attainment. I certainly don't wish to indicate that all educators somehow work to inhibit Appalachian rhetorical sovereignty; that is certainly not true. What does concern me is the prevalence of an attitude, an ideology, so widespread and powerful that it can influence how decision-making powers outside the region institute educational policies that can, themselves, affect attitudes within the region. In other words, how the people who make policy and curricular decisions, as well as those who carry them out, see us (or don't see us) and define our needs affects how we are taught to see ourselves and to define our own needs. For better or for worse.

CHAPTER 7

Categorizing Education

Kim Donehower describes a scene that I would imagine is familiar to many kids in the hills and mountains. A teacher, herself a "local" to the region, describes her daily linguistic battles with students:

> But when they hear [dialect] at home, day in and day out, they come to school and they're wearing that there, and it's hard, you have to go over and go over, repetition, repetition, repetition, to get that—out, and then, I had a child tell me once, I had been hammering on something that I was trying to get into them, one of the students came back and said, "Ms. Sykes," said, "They made fun of me at home, because I did so and so." You know? And I said, "Well you just stick to it because you are right."[1]

And so, by extension, is she.

Again, language is only the tip of the iceberg in terms of what I think of as rhetoric. Rhetoric encapsulates not just word choice and pronunciation but also how we use those words to make sense, for ourselves and others, of the worlds we inhabit. However, language is part of this equation, part of what shapes our discursive "identity kits." When students learn that there are right and wrong ways to use language, specifically when they learn that the language they speak falls into the "wrong" category, the worth of other facets of those identities is likewise called into question. How can we use language to learn and tell our stories if we believe the very language that we use is faulty?

The culture of poverty/deficiency model is a prominent factor in the educational realities many Appalachian students face. As an ideology for educational approaches, it fundamentally promotes, rather than mitigates, inequality. It argues, as historian Ron Eller describes, that under-education is essentially the fault of the poor, who fail to value and take advantage of educational opportunities. It is a feature problematized by his own research and experiences; as he states, in studying Appalachian poverty, "It did not take us long to realize that there was nothing particularly wrong about the attitudes and values of these families struggling with poverty. They did not value education because they themselves were not valued by their schools."[2] Victoria Purcell-Gates agrees; in a two-year-long ethnographic study of an Appalachian family, she discovered a distressing trend among educators to particularly associate "hillbilly language with intractable ignorance."[3] Of course, it isn't students' language alone that must change in order for them to find acceptance within middle-class society; rather, it is what the language represents: they must assimilate to ways of thinking that align with mainstream, middle-class identity. The "good" students will be receptive to attempts at assimilation; the "bad," then, are either unwilling or incapable of such change.

Internalized oppression is a complex dynamic, but one that seems appropriate to consider in terms of Appalachian education. As I noted previously, I was the only Appalachian on the English teaching faculty at my previous community college; this is true for most of the community colleges I've taught in. However, it is distinctly not true for my kindergarten through twelfth-grade experience. Those teaching staffs were mostly made up of locals, yet often their approaches to teaching writing and grammar (or at times, writing *as* grammar) closely mirrored the teacher in Donehower's description. So, the problem isn't anything as simple as "outsiders don't get us, insiders do." (In fact, E. D. Hirsch, one of the first and most vocal proponents of educational standardization and deficit ideology, whose 1987 book *Cultural Literacy: What Every American Needs to Know* provided a philosophical grounding for the educational common-core approach, is from Tennessee.) Knowing what "insider" status even entails is complicated, given the differences in language and culture visible throughout the region. We may have certain linguistic and rhetorical similarities, whether or not some would acknowledge them. But what complicates this is the wide range of attitudes toward those commonalities. Are they good? Bad? How do we decide? Ultimately, it all depends on who you ask. Not many would want to be poor, but some of us do want to be Appalachian.[4] Then again, some of us don't. My concern is with how much schooling, and the mainstream social attitudes that influence schooling, may have to do with where we land on that question.

When I was teaching writing in those Appalachian community colleges, I would survey my students on the first day to ask what they hoped to gain from the class; "to know the right way to write things," or some variation thereof, was a common response. For many of them, the ways that they already wrote were anything but "right," even though follow-up questions revealed that they often couldn't articulate why not. What I want to be sure of is that they've had the chance to critique why they think standardized forms of language and writing are better than others and to fully consider what it is they're being asked to believe when they are told their home versions are subpar. I want them to question, as I wish my grandparents had gotten the chance to do, why they feel like the stories they want to tell aren't stories that can be told in writing.

I have great admiration for public school teachers. Many of them leave home while it's still dark outside and don't get back home until it has fallen dark again, for far less pay than those hours and the tasks they involve ought to warrant. And I think it's important to bear in mind also that many of those teachers aren't allowed to make many choices about what happens in their classrooms. Curriculum is ever more rarely something teachers themselves get to determine. In her 1983 book *Ways with Words* Shirley Brice Heath described doing ethnographic work in the Carolina Piedmont region. The local schools used Heath's work to respond more proactively to the needs of their multicultural and multidialectical student population. Teachers and students worked to analyze and communicate within the multiple discourse communities surrounding them. Teachers, invigorated by the ethnographic methods they were learning from Heath, became "learning researchers," using "ethnographies of communication to build a two-way channel between communities and their classrooms."[5] Students learned "to understand how to make choices among uses of language and to link these choices to life chances,"[6] and the participating teachers gained new knowledge of their students, school communities, and potentials for fostering community health via the educational system.

However, these changes were not lasting. The schools became increasingly required to focus on teaching standardized curriculums, leaving little room for linguistic and cultural exploration. In the epilogue of her book, Heath noted that, as of 1981, the ethnographic methods and place/culture-based work happening in those rural Carolina classrooms had "all but disappeared."[7] Her interviews with the teachers involved revealed that they were increasingly regulated in terms of what to teach, how to teach it, and specifically, how to test it, with required criterion-based, computerized exams. One teacher lamented the attempts to standardize both educational outcomes and, indeed, students themselves:

"They run every kid through the same hierarchy of learning; it's as though everyone developed along the same pattern, and school's gonna make 'em all fit that pattern, like it or not."[8] As another teacher told Heath, "There's no joy left in teaching now."[9]

———

My cousin's boy, David, takes Ohio history in school. I did, too, once upon a time. However, we didn't talk about Appalachia in our Ohio history class. Neither does his. I've looked at Ohio's Common Core standard in social studies, which for his grade:

> focuses on the early development of Ohio and the United States. Students learn about the history, geography, government and economy of their state and nation. Foundations of U.S. history are laid as students study prehistoric Ohio cultures, early American life, the U.S. Constitution, and the development and growth of Ohio and the United States. Students begin to understand how ideas and events from the past have shaped Ohio and the United States today.[10]

Appalachian Ohio is not mentioned, here or in his textbook. Apparently, it has done none of this shaping.

In Language Arts, they study Greco-Roman mythology. They don't study, or even hear about, the *Tain Bo Cuailnge*, the *Acallam na Senórach*, nor of the Celtic fascination with liminalities of thought and expression. They learn duality, category. That is, according to the experts, what they need to know.

———

If all Appalachia is fundamentally no different than mainstream America (only more backward), or if any differences can be explained primarily by poverty (which, in Payne's ideology, produces the same alterations in all peoples and cultures), then the sorts of textbooks I've seen assigned to Appalachian community college students are less problematic. In other words, student texts don't need to acknowledge differences in culture or rhetoric because these differences don't exist. Or, if they do, they exist only as poverty-induced detriments to students' abilities to achieve gainful employment, educational opportunities, and medical care . . . or even to think at all.

For the record, I don't agree with the deficit/poverty model approach to what education is and what it should do. While I recognize that students hope for increased economic prospects from their educations, I have never believed that teaching the language and rhetoric of power requires that other forms be eradicated in, or even absent from, the classroom. Joseph Harris and Min-Zhan Lu have raised prominent critiques of the education-as-mainstream-initiation concept. As Harris notes: "The task facing our students, as Min-Zhan Lu has argued, is not to leave one community in order to enter another, but to reposition themselves in relation to several continuous and conflicting discourses."[11] Whether educators see their role as middle-class-induction or cultural investigation (or both), failing to surface or think critically about what different rhetorics look like or how they work does a disservice to either. My grandparents, many of my students, and even I have felt disconnected from the ways of writing we are taught to think of as good. It was a long time before I began to think about why that was, let alone to *question* what it was schools and society believed I needed to learn. For others, the time for that contemplation may never come.

Textbooks play a distinct role in how students encounter "good" writing and how they are taught to create it. If educators look at Appalachian students as bringing cultural and communicative values to the classroom, then it's worth considering how textbooks might be clashing with students' communicative values in subtle but powerful ways. There are two things, specifically, that I would like to surface as being essentially problematic in the textbook approaches I've encountered. On one hand, many of the textbooks I've seen and used in writing classes rely on distinct categorizations of writing, something that in and of itself can be alienating, and on the other, the specifics of how these categories are defined can be very different from how students have encountered rhetoric on the outside. While I'm not criticizing either the authors of these texts or the teachers who assign them, I do think there's a gap between the assumptions these texts rely on and the population of students expected to benefit from them.

The first assumption I would like to examine is the categorization of knowledge/writing. The textbooks I encountered as a student and a teacher—including the popular *Patterns*, *A Pocketful of Essays*, *Grassroots*, and *At a Glance: Essays*—approached writing by separating it into modes: Narration, Description, Comparison/Contrast, Process Analysis, Classification/Division, Definition, Exemplification, Cause/Effect, and Argument. The problem, as I see it, is not about modes as a philosophy of writing per se. However, what modes do at the root is indicate that good writing is about making distinctions. Students can come to think of writing as boxed up, with each box having a distinct set of instructions. Again, this, in itself, is perhaps not inherently bad. But what concerns me is that it emphasizes a form of categorical thinking that might not come naturally to students or that, according to Appalachian writer Wendell Berry, is not even good for the world at large. The philosophy of categorization, which he calls an aspect of "specialization" thinking, can have widely negative social consequences:

The first, and best known, hazard of the specialist system is that it produces specialists—people who are elaborately and

expensively trained to do one thing. We get into absurdity
very quickly here. There are, for instance, educators who
have nothing to teach, communicators who have nothing to
say, medical doctors skilled at expensive cures for diseases
that they have no skill, and no interest, in preventing. More
common, and more damaging, are the inventors, manufac-
turers, and salesmen of devices who have no concern for the
possible effects of those devices. Specialization is thus seen as
a way of institutionalizing, justifying, and paying highly for
a calamitous disintegration and scattering-out of the various
functions of character: workmanship, care, conscience,
responsibility.[12]

This is a form of thinking that has admittedly given the world
incredible technological and medical advances; as one of my students, who had been born extremely premature, told me, were it
not for specialization thinking and the specialists it produces, he
might not be alive. However, as Berry notes, it has also given us a
world of environmental degradation and social ignorance about
basic principles, in which many people don't know even the basics
of food production or sustainable living because these are
"abdicat[ed] to specialists of various competences and responsibili-
ties [despite being] once personal and universal."[13] By veering too
far into specialization thinking, we and our world have all become
unbalanced.

Yet Payne's culture of poverty model holds that categorical
thinking is essential to cognition and problem-solving, and that is
why it is the domain of the mainstream middle class. To think in
other ways, particularly in the connective, narrative-based way I've
experienced in Appalachia, is to not think at all, at least not seriously or academically. The prevalence of mode-based categorization in introductory college composition textbooks seems, even if
tacitly, to endorse this ideology.

But, according to the culture of poverty model, it's the kind of thinking we need to learn. It is, therefore, acceptable not to raise counterdiscourses in the composition classroom because such countermodels of language or rhetoric would detract from what we need most: the values of the middle class, the mainstream, the keys to assimilation. In the writing classroom, this means that what we learn, if we can manage to, is a categorized discourse of "sequence, order, cause and effect, and a conclusion: all skills necessary for problem-solving [and] inference."[14]

However, what seems to happen in the classroom is rarely ever so clear-cut as this. My sense is that few teachers (whether "insiders" or "outsiders," to Appalachian discourse) and even perhaps few students see what happens in the classroom as the work of cultural assimilation and silencing. Like I said, I would never have started looking if not for Geneva Smitherman. I would never have known to try. So what Appalachian writers may encounter in the mode-based writing classroom is disorienting for reasons they perhaps cannot explain . . . they only feel, like Nathan Shepley's student Matt, oddly distanced from what they are expected to learn and perform.

An emphasis on writing as categorization is potentially problematic, but the definitions those categories receive can also be at odds with the Appalachian rhetorical tradition I've described. The textbooks *Pocketful of Essays* and *At a Glance: Essays*, for example, both take the common approach of splitting writing and rhetoric into separate modes. What is similarly problematic to me is how each of these texts describes these modes. As David Madden's *Pocketful of Essays* describes, "All good narratives center on a conflict (or paradox)."[15] Likewise, Lee Brandon, in *At a Glance: Essays*, specifies that "A narrative is an account of an incident or a series of incidents that make up a complete and significant action"; narratives in their entirety are composed of situation, conflict, struggle, outcome, and meaning, which is stated in a thesis.[16] By this definition, a narrative, a story, is by its nature a function of conflict rather than continuation. But what, I wonder, if the situation *is* the story? I'm thinking, here, of the narratives I've seen from Crooks Harper, Kindness, and some of my students; in other words, what about when our stories focus on the rhythm of days rather than their discordance? Is it not possible to tell a story that has no conflict? Maybe, but apparently not a good one. I think, too, of Brandon's description of the narrative arc in relation to some of those Celtic narratives, such as the *Tain Bo Cuailnge*, which has plenty of conflict, but also has long lists of names and places, as well as digressions into characters' thoughts and experiences, even interrupting battle scenes. A race of storytellers we may be, but I'm not so sure that our way of telling those stories is so easy to pin down and define as the directions about "event" and "conflict" imply.

———

Pap told me once, "I used to know of a woman they said could take the fire out of burns." I imagine this was important, in a time when people's daily lives revolved around open flame in a way they simply do not today—heating, cooking, washing, light: fire was the key to all these things. That burns were common is not surprising. Nor was this style of healing uncommon; I've come to discover that many places had a specific fire healer, one who may or may not have healed any other conditions. Because taking the fire out of burns was concentrated work, it could require its own form of specialization. It took time, energy, and words. The fire healer's art was not possible without words: a Bible verse, specifically, was spoken over the burn. Not everyone had the gift, of course, even with the words. But the healing was not possible without them.

"Did it really work though?" I asked him.

Pap looked thoughtful. "Well, so far as I know, she never got any complaints."

This wasn't a story about a specific event or happening. The burn healing didn't happen just once; there wasn't even a specifically dramatic time he could point out as emblematic of its occurrence. And there was no conflict; on the contrary, this was a story of soothing, acceptance. Yet it was a *story*, and it was one he found worth the telling. Words can do many things. Bind and separate, preserve and destroy, heal and harm. Maybe that's why some people try so hard to put them in labeled boxes. Yet, how could anything so powerful as words not have at least a little mystery?

———

However, I'm not sure that narrative is the only form of writing in which I see ideological discordance between the textbooks I encountered and my own background as a writer. It's easy to get the sense from many such textbooks that argument is perceived as the highest form of academic writing. I've already discussed some of the ways in which academic argument, as the forthright attempt to convince readers of a specific point, stated clearly in a thesis,[17] has the potential to jar students who share the sense of Appalachian rhetoric I've been describing. As Brandon explains, argument is essentially persuasion over a fundamental issue; a well-structured argument is composed of background, a proposition, refutation, and support, which in itself consists of "sound reasoning . . . appropriate facts, examples, statistics, and opinions of authorities."[18] Of course, when we apply these factors to Appalachia, ain't a one of them as simple as it sounds.

Kim Donehower writes an excellent analysis of James Moffett's *Storm in the Mountains: A Case Study of Censorship, Conflict, and Consciousness* that I think has relevance here. Donehower describes Moffett's book as a work that "pits the academic literacy professional against the supposedly 'anti-intellectual' non-professional," exploring a situation from the 1970s in which Kanawha County, West Virginia, "banned a set of textbook materials for high school

English classes that (Moffett) had edited."[19] I have a familial interest in Kanawha County. When my three-times great-grandfather
enlisted in the Union Army, his unit formed part of the Kanawha
Brigade, which protected the Union flank at the Battle of Antietam.
Moffett also seems to enter the region with battle on his mind; he
"repeatedly tries to convince his informants of the wrongness of
their stance. Using the didactic rhetoric of Socratic education,
Moffett asks the kind of leading questions a teacher asks a student
(when the teacher already has the 'right' answer to the question
firmly in mind)."[20] To his astonishment, these "anti-intellectuals"
just won't play ball. He is baffled by their responses to his leading
questions, responses that, as Donehower notes, rely heavily on
"scriptural quotations, parables, and local anecdotes and analo-
gies"[21] and at times seem to Moffett entirely irrelevant to the issue
at hand. Sometimes, Moffett's informants are "able to end up
exactly opposite of where Moffett has been trying to lead [them]."[22]
In other words, Moffett simply isn't able, through traditional academic rhetoric, to "convince" his Appalachian audience of anything. The result is that Moffett decrees the populace to be suffering
from "'agnosis'—a term he coins to mean, essentially, the desire to
be ignorant."[23] This, it seems, is their punishment for not agreeing
with Moffett's rhetoric . . . or, as it may be, for having a different
one.

While I, personally, am vociferously anti-censorship—not all of
us think the same, after all—I agree with Donehower that:

> Far from demonstrating some kind of backward mental
> state, I believe the Kanawha County residents displayed
> canny rhetorical skills that they used to try to protect them-
> selves, their culture, and their worldview from Moffett, who
> would label them ignorant unless they agreed to critique
> their sacred texts, relinquish their way of looking at the
> world, and generally come around to his way of thinking.[24]

I find leading questions and the "Ha! caught you out" impulse that seems to underlie them extremely irritating, even dishonest. Maybe that reaction is individual, maybe it's cultural. But I can tell you, as anti-censorship as I am, if I had talked to Moffett and he pulled one of those leading questions on me, I might have disagreed with him on principle. Though I might not have put it as "disagreement" in a way he recognized: I might just have smiled and told him a story about my grandparents.

Essentially, I want to consider the possibility that the academic argument described in these textbooks, specifically what it presents as "fact," "support," and "logic," can mean different, more complex things than what is often assumed. It can, in some circumstances, feel like an attack, even if the attackers don't always see that as their purpose, and the attackees don't always have practice in describing what is being threatened.

———

So, I could simply say that I advocate surfacing cultural dynamics like these to help students better understand why they may feel alienated by writing instruction and to help them work past it in order to better succeed in their composition classes. But I want to consider, also, that the presence or absence of discussion about Appalachian rhetoric and culture might be important for more reasons than just to help these students understand and master standardized forms.

In chapter one, I described getting peer feedback on a paper from a peer reviewer who couldn't see how sustainability and Appalachian culture were conceptually linkable. It was back when I was a master's student, in a paper where I first articulated an idea that would play over in my head steadily in the years to come: that if we want sustainability in Appalachia, we need to bring Appalachian culture into the region's classrooms. My reader also asked, in his final reflection, another important question: "Why do we need to talk about Appalachia in our classes? Especially since our focus is on providing an up-to-date, global education?" In other words, what is Appalachia's value? Its worth? Particularly in college, where the educational focus on the global, the fresh and cutting edge, seems so at odds with how Appalachia is defined?

Since then, my sense is that the binary between global and local is being productively questioned in many educational arenas, but I'm not convinced that all Appalachian students are yet feeling the effects of that complexity. To answer those questions, as well as I can from my perspective today, I say this: Appalachia belongs in the classroom because it can help to both validate and complicate identity. It can help students figure out what pressures come from their communities and which come from outside them, which pressures they want to respond to and which they want to resist. We can help them see that the place-connection their rhetorics may promote isn't necessarily a bad thing. Loving their communities isn't something to be ashamed of. And by learning to interact with varied forms of discourse, they can help shape themselves and their communities in productive ways. This is a reality demonstrated by Katherine Kelleher Sohn, whose Appalachian interview subjects completed college and stayed in, rather than left, their home communities. Each has used some element of their expanded literacy practices to benefit those communities. Likewise, Jennifer Beech argues that even Appalachian students who don't complete their degrees benefit from rhetoric and writing instruction that incorporates their community needs and backgrounds. As she notes, "A student who took that composition course but who later drops out of college before completing his degree may have gained rhetorical strategies for addressing those within positions of power in his home community (teachers, school board or city council members, a supervisor)."[25] They can gain a clearer idea of what their needs are, who they want to be, what shapes their realities, and what power they have to reshape them.

Appalachia did appear in classrooms at my alma mater, the college where I completed both my undergraduate and graduate degrees. Some of my English teachers there were the first I encountered who encouraged me to study my cultural background. However, these teachers were individuals, not the system, and often it seems the system takes the deficit definition of Appalachia for granted. I remember looking through the student newspaper during the last semester of my graduate work, to find a feature length article entitled "Courses Examine Culture and Setbacks of Life in Appalachia." Setbacks. Of course. That's what life, what culture, in Appalachia is, apparently: one long, long setback.

As an institution, the college seemed to accept Appalachia as deficit: solve or ignore, but don't celebrate. For example, the report entitled "Appalachian Perspectives at Ohio University" pointed out that in 2006, the university had the opportunity to host the Appalachian Studies Association's annual conference. They declined. Also, despite being the only major research institution in my part of Appalachia, the school still does not offer an Appalachian Studies program. Another recent tuition hike resulted in vocal displeasure among the student body; the cost has certainly risen above what many within the region can afford. When questioned about the financial repercussions for students, one administrator said that students who disliked the costs could "vote with their feet" and leave. As Todd Snyder could've told him, it's not that simple, when the culture teaches us to value home and family and when that particular college is, for local students, the only educational resource in proximity to those. I can't say for certain, but I doubt the administrator who made that statement was much aware of Appalachian cultural influences. Appalachia certainly wasn't specified in his comments. For plenty of people, the concepts of "university" and "Appalachia" don't even inhabit the same world. They are different modes, so to speak.

I wondered, at one point, what the runaway success of *The Hunger Games* would mean for a widespread conversation about Appalachia. My interpretation of the book was that it was a stark appraisal of cultural values and ideologies, taking the harshest elements of modern American consumer culture and ramping them up to their most destructive conclusion: where sparkle, appearance, and fame are valued above all and where a privileged elite make the death and despair of the poor into *Survivor*-style, reality-TV entertainment. In the story, this system is disrupted by the efforts of a girl from District 12—a futuristic Appalachia—whose actions and values embody Appalachian ideals of self-sufficiency, bravery, and family loyalty.[26] Katniss as a character is held up for our admiration as she defies and defeats the simultaneous shallowness and disdain of a hyper-consumerist culture. *What will people think of that?* I wondered.

I needn't have. Consumer culture, apparently, can afford to ignore its critiques. For example, Cover Girl cosmetics followed up the success of the film adaptations (and what has become a *Hunger Games* franchise) with a line of Capital and District-inspired cosmetics, so that the consumer can better emulate the extreme futuristic fashions displayed by the film's ruling elite. (Despite the fact that, as the story makes clear, these are the people we are NOT supposed to want to emulate.) And, I've come to understand, relatively few seem to interpret District 12, and by extension the heroic Katniss Everdeen, as Appalachian at all. As I've noted, one of my classes was startled to learn that author Suzanne Collins ever intended such a correlation. District 12 wasn't evident as Appalachia, despite the fact that Collins even calls it that at one point in the book,[27] because *The Hunger Games* was set in the future. Yes. And Appalachia, if it exists, is eternally the past.

Why, then, does it matter that Appalachia has no place in most classrooms? In our sense of multicultural education? What does Appalachia have to offer? These are tricky questions and ones that I probably wouldn't try to answer if it weren't for the fact that I am so often asked them directly. Ultimately, I don't like the thought that I'm answering for others, so I will answer, instead, for myself: here is what I think Appalachia has to offer. You can, of course, disagree.

I remember Loyal Jones's *Appalachian Values* as the first book I ever encountered to put in writing regional cultural traits that were, at least in some views, positive rather than negative. According to Jones, the elements Appalachian culture demonstrates include independence, yet also neighborliness; humility, yet also pride; and a sense of humor interspersed with tragedy.[28] Just looking at this list, I'm dumbfounded at how often Appalachian culture is coded as "simple"—seems to me like you can't get much more complicated than a culture that combines all of these. Because cultural definition is so complicated and because making concrete statements about these values can erase those who don't fit the parameters, some people advocate abandoning the attempt all together. However, if we are to think about regional differences (and the rhetorics promoting them) as something other than deficits, it seems to me that thinking about these ideas can be worthwhile. Yet they must always remain flexible and tentative; intersectionality is needed to avoid the very erasure of differences within groups that projects such as Jones's can be critiqued for making.

And so, my tentative and flexible reading of Appalachian culture, something encouraged and shaped by the stories we tell and how we tell them, is of a way of life that *can* teach us all something valuable in the modern world. Perhaps what Appalachian culture does best, at least as I've experienced it, is create a sense of ourselves as shaped by place. I have learned to rhetorically conceive of spaces and the peoples who live in them as intertwined, even interdependent.

It's not a simple concept, and valuing place doesn't mean Appalachia doesn't have environmental problems; we certainly do. Ron Eller, in an interview with journalist David DeWitt, makes a compelling case that the modern idea of economic growth as incompatible with environmental health is a fiction encouraged by extractive industries and the government. Governmental War on Poverty programs have been designed to create jobs but not, at the same time, protect the land. I think again about my neighbors, who have signed fracking leases but also demanded water protections. What, I wonder, would those War on Poverty programs have looked like if we could have designed them ourselves? That we didn't, of course, is itself probably the point.

It is this value for place and our ability to see it as part of our families, part of ourselves, that I would posit our rhetoric preserves and promulgates. It's a value that, in a world where people seem to increasingly ache for roots,[29] is worth wider consideration. It is this value that can enrich our multicultural world, if we learn to be seen and to see ourselves as part of it. But it is also this value that, without forthright considerations of how our rhetorics work and why we needn't simply think of them as "incorrect," could bleed out of us.

————

Strangely enough, I sometimes find it easier to explain what I'm *not* trying to say than what I am. And I want to say that I do *not* wish, with this exploration, to argue that all Appalachians value the same things, or that our students should not be exposed to ideologies or concepts that run counter to those they bring with them to the classroom. It is, after all, a central tenet of education to expose students to different ideas, experiences, and histories. Nor do I wish to implicate all textbooks, or all teachers, in some sort of a conspiracy to undermine Appalachian culture or rhetoric. Appalachian rhetoric and culture are not monoliths. My concern is for something much subtler: that when students aren't allowed to investigate their own rhetorical and cultural genealogies, they don't see exactly what it is that is being undermined or that undermining is happening at all. That when we learn in school not that we have a discourse but that we simply speak and write incorrectly, or when we fail to learn that there might be a reason why we want to tell particular stories in particular ways, undermining happens, the result being loss, for us and for the world.

Chapter 8

Education and Rhetorical Identity

I have an image in my head of one of my Great-Grandma Carpenter's quilts. This quilt is, in various ways, both how I've been writing and what I've been writing about. According to Fawn Valentine, "Scotch-Irish quiltmakers appear more absorbed in process, cutting and sewing, than in visual arrangement."[1] I see this in the quilt, with its haphazard arrangement of patterned cloth and bright, sometimes clashing colors. I think about her quilt when I recall Robin Chapman Stacey's description of Celtic law texts, which didn't just explicate specific laws, but also explored the process through which individual jurists drew conclusions.[2] This book is my process of thinking about how my identity, and potentially those of other Appalachian peoples, has been influenced by regional rhetoric, its history, and its reception in classrooms. In quilting my answer, I've chosen a theme, a pattern, a basic structural outline to follow, but even I wonder if what falls within those lines might come across as a bit chaotic. That certainly seems to be the case with my great-grandmother's quilt: the choices of cloth and color blur the distinctions between pattern and chaos. She also sewed into this quilt a pattern of webs and waves; it's a choice that makes it an even more apt metaphor for my sense of how our regional rhetoric functions.

At least some dimension of Appalachian rhetoric, as I have historicized and described it, is itself a study in pattern and chaos.

Boundaries between self and community, land and people, history and future, are routinely nudged or outright collapsed. This form of writing can defy organizational description; stories, poetry, recipes, images, document scans, can all blend together in the service of explaining the workings of the writer's mind and the places and peoples who shaped it. Reading a text written like the autobiographies I've described feels a bit like looking at my Great-Grandma Carpenter's quilt. There is a theme here in her quilt, but within that pattern is a little bit of everything that she thinks fits. I probably wouldn't have chosen the same patterns, arrangements, or colors were I in her place. I can only trust that these mattered to her, that the process of composing was as important as the end result, and yet that by preserving the quilt, she believed she was conveying something worth seeing.

———

My Great-Grandma Carpenter's given name was Alta, but around here that got pronounced Alty. So did most names ending in *a*; when I was little, my grandparents' pet name for me was Matilda . . . or rather, Matildy. I never did know why they picked that name, since it bears no resemblance to my given name, and now I never will.

Alty used to tell stories about her childhood. We think. See, Alty was a bit of a talker, not so much as her sister was, so I'm told, but still perfectly willing to share what was on her mind. The problem was that, at least toward the end of her life, hardly anyone could understand her when she talked. She'd been pretty much a lifelong snuff dipper, and even in old age retained the habit of talking like she was working around a mouthful of snuff. The result was a sort of throaty "Murblemurblemurble" that wasn't exactly easy to understand. However, she was rarely asked to repeat herself; there were few of us brave enough to do that. I imagine she would've taken it as a sign you weren't listening, and I don't think anyone was eager to take that risk. It was best to keep on Alty's good side.

There's a story Mom likes to tell about herself listening to Alty tell a story. Mom had long ago learned that you sometimes have to sacrifice comprehension for peace and was just nodding along when Alty said something that sounded like:

"Murblemurblemurble SHIT IN THE CROCK A-BUTTER murblemurblemurble."

Alty could certainly be clear when it counted. Although Mom never did find out what the rest of that story was about.

I don't suppose it matters, though. By this point, Alty herself has *become* the story, almost a legend. In telling her stories, as we do, to her great-great-grandchildren, I've come to believe we're doing something more than just acquainting them with their ancestry; we're telling them that this acquaintance and way of making it *matters*. (My cousin's daughter Emmy was born after Alty had died, but she knows her well, specifically because we've told her so often that she's inherited Alty's temper. Her mom even refers to Emmy's tantrums as "Alty-sodes.") Maybe they won't remember the stories themselves—I'm certain there are plenty I've forgotten. But, if they learn that stories are powerful, if they see that stories can help them think about who they are and where they come from, then that will be enough. These stories might, then, do for them what they did for me.

This quilt is also what I've been writing *about*, in the sense that I look at it and see a vital thread in my identity, in my community's potential for rhetorical sovereignty. Alty, as a quilter, made her own choices, for her own reasons, and expected them to be respected (which, in our family and our quilt-loving region, I would say they are). When I go to the Folk Festival's annual quilt display, with its combination of historical and modern quilts, and when I read Fawn Valentine's book on Appalachian quilting traditions, I see a thread that runs through much of this geographic cradle of hills and mountains. What I learned from Valentine's book in particular is that my great-grandmother's quilts connected her to a history of hills, mountains, and people across an ocean, something I'm not sure even she fully realized.

———

In that class I taught on Appalachian rhetoric, a class that happened to coincide with an election cycle, I asked my students to consider why Appalachia hasn't previously been seen as a regional power-block. In other words, why did we never before hear about politicians in major elections courting the Appalachian vote? (Ironically, I think that the presidential candidates in a more recent election cycle *did* try to appeal to Appalachia, with varying amounts of cynicism and with drastically varying results.) One student suggested that maybe not enough people in Appalachia voted, another that maybe they didn't donate enough campaign funds to be seen as important. Or, another suggested, maybe Appalachians were just too individualistic to be seen as a people whose voices could unite to have power. It was the last point that captured me. I said, somewhat thinking aloud, "Imagine if Appalachia saw itself as a united front for social action; like, if Appalachia decided collectively to do something about unequal school funding. I don't think such a thing has ever really been considered." Another student raised his hand. "So why is it that Appalachia can unite for bad reasons but not good ones?" he asked.

I wasn't sure what to make of this. "Explain that question a bit more."

He shrugged. "You know, they're fine with getting together to form the KKK and neo-Nazi groups."

I tried to explain to him that Appalachia was not actually united behind the KKK or neo-Nazi groups, that participation in these groups was not at all regionally specific to here. However, it's a powerful image: there seems to be a concern that when Appalachians unite politically, it's to rally against social progress, civil rights, even their own best economic and environmental interests. But is it true? Can this even happen when most of us have never had the opportunity to reflect on our identities as Appalachians, let alone to build coalitions around those identities for *any* reasons?

———

To consider these questions, I find myself looking, as I so often do, into my experiences with rhetoric. My student's question has stayed with me: with so much cultural emphasis on individualism and self-sufficiency, is group identity in Appalachia even possible or desirable? I would answer that question today by saying that Appalachian rhetoric, as I've experienced it, has the potential for embracing both individual and group identity, depending on how we approach it. I can present myself and my thoughts as those of an individual, but I am kept always cognizant of how that individual identity has been shaped by interactions with family and community. I can approach "argument" through narrative as something that encourages connection and acceptance but doesn't insist on them. I can explain what Appalachia means to me; what I can't promise is what it means to others. Rather, I can invite others to see themselves in my definition, or, whether they do or not, to make use of my thinking as a model on which to undertake their own. We stay our individual selves in this rhetorical tradition I'm unearthing, with our individual right to either claim or disclaim the influences that affect our identities. I don't want to insist that anyone, including my regional students, claim an Appalachian identity. Rather, what I want to show them is how I've come to claim my own and how I've felt empowered by that claiming. I want them to see that their identities, as individual as they may seem, have potentially been shaped in similar ways as those of the people around them. I want them to consider that the ways we come to see ourselves and interpret our lives is cultural rather than natural, and therefore we have power over that process. But only if we can see it. And only if we can see ourselves as tied up in the same struggles.

There are, of course, dangers implicit in seeking cultural group identity. On one hand, identity politics can create "Groups [that] tend to remain separate, focused on their own issues and concerns, sometimes competing with each other for recognition and resources."[3] An Appalachian group identity that does not see itself as intersectional, as interconnected with other peoples, other places, as diverse and complex, would likely cause all of us more harm than good.

I am drawn, therefore, to the definition posed by feminist theorists Gwyn Kirk and Margo Okazawa-Rey of identity-*based* politics, which "has a strong identity component and also a broader view that allows people to make connections to other groups and issues."[4] In examining my Appalachian rhetorical identity, and encouraging similar examinations by others in the region, I am seeking such a possibility: a group identity that encourages coalition and empowerment, without the concretizing of definition that creates disconnection or divisiveness. Good thing, in this sense, that our rhetoric has possibilities for boundary-crossing, not just categorization, sewn right in. As Todd Snyder has noted, Appalachian identity can be very much a matter of individual self-identification and definition.[5] This, rather than a weakness, can be a strength in allowing us to achieve identity-based politics without exclusion . . . if, of course, we can reach a point at which Appalachian identity is presented as a possible and beneficial identity to claim.

Ultimately, I'm positing that a group identity for Appalachia, composed of individuals who have the ability and willingness to think critically about themselves and others, can offer more benefits than drawbacks, for reasons of both self-esteem and power. Let's return to Lyons's definition of rhetorical sovereignty: "the inherent right of peoples to determine their own communicative needs and desires . . . to decide for themselves the goals, modes, styles, and languages of public discourse . . . rhetorical sovereignty requires of writing teachers more than a renewed commitment to listening and learning; it also requires a radical rethinking of how and what we teach as the written word at all levels of schooling."[6] In other words, the latter (a renewed thinking about how we teach writing) can help us achieve the former (our right to determine our own discursive identities). In Appalachia, I consider the latter to be particularly essential in helping us to see ourselves as a people, to explore and surface our linguistic, rhetorical, cultural, and historical connections in ways we rarely have the opportunity to do. From my perspective, all of these issues are bound up together in our experience of formal education.

———

I learned at a fairly young age that my grandmother hadn't finished school. This was never a secret. She had grown up as part of a family of sharecroppers over around Calais (pronounced Kay-liss), in Monroe County, with most of her family members born, raised, and buried within walking distance. But Grandma dropped out of school to go north and found work in a grocery store up near Ravenna. She told me how the stores worked back then, how kids would bring their mothers' shopping lists, and she would go find all the things on them while the children waited up front. Grandma didn't stay away from home long, and the cousin she had originally gone with had come back even sooner, out of homesickness.

Grandma and I used to take long walks when I was little, and it was during one of our walks that I first learned about her educational and work history. It took a while before I understood how to reconcile the grandma I knew, who seemed to me to know so much, who it seemed could just about name every flower we passed on our evening walks, who read and told good stories, with the high school dropout.

"Your parents just let you quit school?" I asked.

"It wasn't such a big thing. Going to work made more sense," she explained.

I learned, eventually, to question how and what I learned in school. I learned to see that education and school were not synonymous. I learned that sometimes the immediate needs of your family mattered much more than schooling did, or, at least, that the school system could matter far less. That this separation of "school" and "life" was possible is, to me, part of the problem. But it is a problem that can be mitigated, as place-based and critical approaches to education have shown.

My grandmother could tell a good story, but she never felt comfortable writing one down. She certainly never thought of herself as smart. I understand now that school, as she experienced it, had a great deal to do with both of these.

———

If we look at a map of the Appalachian region, we can see immediately that it is vast. Are all people within this region culturally identical? No. Will all of these people self-identify as Appalachian? No. But think, for a moment, just how many schools exist within this expanse and how many students are learning to read and write within them. Think how many of us have taught or are teaching the students of Appalachia, perhaps without even recognizing it. In my experience as a teacher at three community colleges within the region, nearly all of my students were "locals." In other words, they were the very people for whom considerations of Appalachian identity and rhetoric are most relevant. Even as a teacher at a major research university located in Appalachia, I had a small but consistent stream of regional undergrads—I, once upon a time, was one myself. Yet considerations of Appalachian identity don't only matter for those who are born and bred within the region. I also thought of my non-local students, when they entered my class, as entering an Appalachian classroom: most of my university students came from outside the region but were now living here, although few, I learned, even consciously realized it. "How many of you knew when you came to this university that you were moving to Appalachia?" I would ask my classes. Very, very few did. Yet I wanted them to realize it, as I want all people to think, and care, about where they plant their lives. Because, if Appalachian rhetorical sovereignty is going to happen, then we need to talk about what *living in* Appalachia means, whether or not we were born here.

There are many things happening in rhetoric and composition pedagogy that I heartily endorse for Appalachian classrooms and that I wish I had experienced myself as a student. What I'd like to see are two things, both based in the regional realities of daily life: 1) that rhetorical and identity-based pedagogical practices more routinely reach Appalachian classrooms and 2) that "Appalachian" as an identity-marker becomes a regular concept in these classrooms, one that students and teachers have the space and encouragement to explore and critique.

Make no mistake, these kinds of things are happening in parts of the region, and they succeed in varied ways at making Appalachian language, culture, rhetoric, and students' identities part of the educational experience. Specifically, they make *place* an integral part of students' educational experiences. It is because of what these programs offer that I want to see them happen more regularly and widely.

The history of place-based education in Appalachia is actually far deeper than many realize, stretching as far back as Elsie Clapp's work with the school in Arthurdale, West Virginia, during the Great Depression. Clapp utilized local culture, skills, and language to create a place-centered curriculum, the goal of which was to bolster a sense of regional self-sufficiency that was being drained by life in West Virginia's coal camps.[7] Clapp was an early believer in the value local rhetorical and linguistic traditions could play in the classroom. Though she initially approached writing instruction as inextricable from the teaching of the "correct form," she came to recognize her students' rhetorics and language as a means of "sharing, of voicing, of recording. As a form of experiencing . . . in a special sense, history."[8] Given that Clapp's educational purpose was rooted in history, in reawakening local life skills such as farming and crafting that had once provided a means of living outside the coal industry, this recognition was important. Clapp consciously wanted to maintain rather than change traditional ways of life in rural West Virginia. To a degree, she succeeded in revitalizing these traditions; these skills continued to be used productively by many participants "for the rest of their lives, carrying on the handcraft tradition of the community years after"[9] the project formally ended. But end it did, in part because it lost wider federal support.

However, Clapp's curriculum and value for place-based learning proved a valuable starting point for other projects. Some of the earliest and still best proof that this approach works came from Shirley Brice Heath's study, conducted in the Carolina Piedmont region during the 1970s and described in her book *Ways with Words*. Heath conducted a meticulous study of how "home" literacy shaped and prepared students from diverse backgrounds for the literacies they would encounter in school. Local educators began working with Heath to train students as ethnographers, investigators "of their own and others' interactions . . . to put to use knowledge about the different ways of learning and using language which existed in the communities of their region."[10] In doing so, these teachers showed that local needs and strengths could be taken seriously in the classroom and that school could be a place where students learned to solve the problems confronting them in their daily lives.

In one project, elementary students were asked to "imagine they had just been set down as strangers in their own community"[11] in order to investigate how local people's ideas about agriculture differed from the scientific knowledge they learned in class, as well as to consider why these differences might occur. In order to do this successfully, students needed to think about what made communication with the "experts" in their communities work (or not). The conclusion of the unit was a class-authored "science book" that drew from local knowledge and included the stories and life histories told to them by local farmers. This project allowed students to think across disciplinary boundaries (between English, communication, and science), while also encouraging students to value the local expertise available outside classroom walls. Significantly, students were able to think about both local knowledges and styles of communication—they not only gained data, they also learned about how it is conveyed through stories and explanations of experience. They then translated these into the types of academic discourse they encountered in textbooks, including researching and compiling comparative charts translating interview data into scientific reasoning.[12] In other words, they learned to consider what it means to be literate in the life of their community, by critically examining what issues exist (in this case, agricultural/environmental) and how to go about learning and affecting them. They learned that the communication methods in their Appalachian community, predominated by storytelling and the personalization of information (they couldn't learn about farming's best practices without learning about the lives of the practitioners), were different than academic styles of knowledge creation, but not less valid.

While Heath doesn't expand on what this means in terms of Appalachian literacy, it is nonetheless potentially revealing about how Appalachian discourse creates and sustains the sense of place-connection with which it is attributed: the conveyance of fact (agricultural data) is inextricable from narrative autobiography (the farmers' life stories and experiences on the land). This is a significant rhetorical connection: people and place are linked through the personalized stories used to teach children. Through this lens, it is easier to understand how regional students can perceive the academic discourse of textbooks as abstract or disconnected from their lives,[13] if for no other reason than rhetorical presentation. Rather than choosing either regional or academic as the exclusive discourse of the classroom, this example shows that students can become more aware of both, as well as how discourses function, by having differences brought to the forefront for exploration.

This pedagogical approach succeeded at multiple levels: for students, for teachers, and for their communities. At a time when school desegregations were bringing more diversity to the classroom than ever before, these children learned "to understand how to make choices among uses of language and to link these choices to life chances."[14] The participating teachers gained new knowledge of their students, school communities, and opportunities for fostering community health via the educational system. Yet, like the Arthurdale project, this place-based, ethnographic approach to learning suffered from a lack of support at state and national levels, leading it to be replaced with a focus on test-based standardization. For more community-specific changes in school curricula to be seeded is one thing, but to take solid root is apparently quite another.

One project focusing on place-based writing in Appalachia that has endured has been the Foxfire project, begun in Rabun County,

Georgia, in 1966. Foxfire began as a student-run folklore maga-
zine, in which students interviewed local community members in
order to write articles about traditions, skills, and stories. Foxfire's
creator Eliot Wigginton posed that the project allowed students to
see themselves as part of their communities, as agents who "can act
responsibly and effectively rather than being always acted upon,"
and to view English studies as a means of "reaching out and touch-
ing people with words, sounds, and visual images."[15] While
Foxfire-style projects continue to be found scattered throughout
the region (and, indeed, the country), it is the exception rather
than the rule. Educational professor Sharon Teets advocates
Foxfire's revitalization in Appalachia, specifically because of what
it can mean for teaching: a way of making the classroom student-
centered, active, and critically responsive to local needs. As Teets
writes, "The approach, if used faithfully and over time, has the real
potential to empower the youngest citizens of the Appalachian
region to become increasingly decisive about how their lives will be
led."[16] I would add that gaining this decisiveness requires a wider,
more sustained classroom focus on rhetoric itself, in terms of how
it shapes us and our interpretations, than what we are currently
seeing.

There are projects working currently to make place-based education a reality at various levels of schooling. Adriana Trigiani's
Origin Project in Big Stone Gap, Virginia, "seeks to inspire students to find their voices through the craft of writing about their
Appalachian origins," with the premise that "When we connect to
the stories of our past, we are able to build our dreams for the
future." The connections of place, stories, history, and future are all
threads I see in Appalachian rhetorical traditions, and Trigiani's
educational program brings these traditions formally into classrooms throughout a four-county expanse of southwest Virginia.
Likewise, the Appalachian Writing Project, founded in 2000 at The
University of Virginia's College at Wise, works in part to "convince

teachers to take into account the deep, abiding influence of place"
in their students' outlooks, language, and writing, something the
director, Amy Clark, wants to see them "begin teaching about . . .
in elementary school." These programs are happening because
teachers and writers in Appalachia recognize their importance.
However, they aren't reaching all of us, not yet. What we need is
more of these projects (and other similar ones) and for them to
continue long enough that they become part of our "story" of education, our sense of what school can and should do for our
communities.

What does a place-centered writing classroom look like, then?
What can teachers do "on Monday morning" to help students
achieve the kinds of critical rhetorical awareness I and others are
advocating? It's a question I've pondered over and experimented
with in multiple ways. The first attempt I ever made in this direction was a brief unit I was able to work into my community college
syllabus, which I entitled the "Language Analysis Essay."
Pedagogically, this project stems from theorists and practitioners
like Wheeler and Swords, who advocate contrastive analysis (teaching students to examine the differences between dialects) in order
to be better able to code-switch (meaning, to use the dialect that
best fits particular needs or situations). I took as my exigency the
fears I noticed among some students that their native dialects,
mostly Appalachian in origin, made them "sound stupid." The
project started out quite informally; I asked students to study and
keep journals about the ways their dialects altered (or didn't) in
different surroundings or situations. It eventually morphed into a
more formal report, in which students noted the location, subject,
and audiences of these language-use situations. I wanted them to
consider their language uses in terms of linguistic features such as
phonology (including words that might be pronounced or spelled
differently here than in other areas, such as *crick* for *creek* and
worsh for *wash)*, lexicon (such as words/usages that are acceptable

in the local dialect, but not necessarily in standard English; for example, "you'uns"), and grammar. My ultimate goal was that they start to see language as situational, to see that their non-standard dialects did in fact "fit" better in certain situations. As my own experience as a teacher has broadened, I've realized that what I was asking them to consider was the concept of discourse communities, different "ways of being in the world"[17] that can change based on our surroundings, purposes, and the identities we assume in different situations. Discourse community differences seemed at root a far fairer way of looking at linguistic difference than the simple "right" and "wrong" many of us were used to.

My students' language analysis work did not take place at the same school as the Banned Terms Project, but that didn't mean attitudes were not the same. At one point, after we had done a couple of sessions discussing language analysis and situation, two of my students came to class bursting to tell me what had happened in the math course they were taking together. Their teacher had publicly shamed a student for using a double-negative ("weren't none," specifically). One of my students had raised her hand and informed the instructor that the student's usage was in fact not "wrong." The construction "weren't none" was actually a common and accepted usage in local speech; it was only, perhaps, not the most fitting language choice for this particular situation, given the apparent expectations. Her teacher was curious about where she got that idea. She told him, "It's what we're learning in our English class."

My student said her math teacher looked at her for a long moment. Then he said, "Your English teacher ought to be fired."

I think I understand his opinion. If what English teachers are supposed to be doing is "correcting" students' discourse so that they can escape poverty, what I was doing instead, in his view, was keeping them incorrect and thereby trapped in the mire. Despite his opinion, my students seemed quite proud of themselves. Hell, I was rather proud, too. Because my student made a choice in that moment not to simply follow the status quo; she thought about what she valued in language, and she shared that value with someone else. Even if he wasn't willing to agree.

However, while I hope that this project had a positive effect on my students' linguistic outlooks, I don't think it really addressed the issues that concern me now regarding Appalachian rhetorical sovereignty. For one thing, I don't think I did enough to incorporate language use into a more holistic sense of rhetoric; as I hope I have shown, I think there is more to Appalachian senses of cultural identity and communication than the surface features of language. And, while the ability to self-consciously evaluate situations and code-switch in response is undoubtedly valuable, I don't think I pushed far enough in asking my students to resist the insistent pressures that told them their home language "sounded stupid," or that I did enough to encourage them to critique these attempts at cultural alienation and claim ownership over the narrative of their identities. Why is your language "stupid?" I should have asked. Who says so? Why do you believe them? Why do we speak and write the way we do? Where does it come from? What does it achieve? Who else speaks and writes this way? *What do we want from writing, and why?*

In my profession, I often hear stories about the writers who change lives because they make us look at the world differently. Just as important, I've found, are those who make me look at myself differently, who rearrange something I've thought I understood, or hadn't thought about at all, about who or why I am. One was Geneva Smitherman, who taught me to look for a cultural history in my casual usage of "we was." Another was Helen Fox.

Fox's book *Listening to the World: Cultural Issues in Academic Writing* opens with the story of a visit to an American college class by a West African praise singer. Despite all parties conversing in standard English, the students were unable to understand the speaker, whose answers to their questions, it seemed to them, were "totally off the point."[18] Fox draws from this, and continues throughout her book to explain, that *logic* is ultimately cultural, and the ways we use rhetoric to make logical points can differ widely. It was from Fox that I began to wonder about the possibility that Appalachian students may write in ways that are similar to what Fox calls "World Majority Students."[19] While mainstream American students are often raised in "a process of both formal and informal socialization" to value "literal meanings and precise definitions and explicit statements of cause and effect . . . writing sparsely and directly, without embellishments or digressions, beginning each paragraph or section with a general analytical statement,"[20] the same is not necessarily true for all the students entering schools and colleges. The style of writing Fox ascribes to "mainstream" American students is what she calls Western European; this is problematic if we look at some styles of Appalachian rhetoric as descended from Celtic influences, which were also born in Western Europe but have few commonalities to the style she describes. Perhaps our rhetoric is also Western European in origin, but it can at times look nothing like the sparse and direct style of writing American schools value. Thus Appalachia is, again, linguistically erased, lumped in with a very different way of communicating and thereby in comparison described as *wrong* rather than *different*. Nonetheless, were it not for Fox's book, this in itself is a consideration I might never have come to see.

Fox puts forward the notion that by surfacing cultural difference in classrooms, we as instructors both help students better master the forms of academic writing they encounter, to "help [them] cope within the system as it exists,"[21] and also acknowledge "to students and to ourselves, that other reasonable, logical ways of seeing the world exist." For academia to help, rather than inhibit, Appalachian rhetorical sovereignty, this is an acknowledgment that must occur, and for it to occur, an even more preliminary acknowledgment must take place: that Appalachia is cultural, that the difficulties our writers face are, at least potentially, rooted in differing cultural assumptions, values, and definitions . . . in other words, in rhetoric. And that how we use and are used by rhetoric can mean something for how we learn to be in the world.

Recent pedagogical work in Appalachia is demonstrating that this kind of local awareness is fruitful and important; it has the power to shape how students feel about themselves, their communities, and their roles as citizens. Yet it is not enough to simply ask students to write down their experiences. They need, also, to critique them, to think about what shapes those experiences and how they can respond to that shaping. Amy Azano's 2011 article entitled "The Possibilities of Place: One Teacher's Use of Place-Based Instruction for English Students" described an eighth-grade class in which place deliberately shaped instructional choices, including the choice of reading assignments, writing assignments, and topics for class discussion. Azano found that the class succeeded in giving students the "license to create their own concepts of place" while identifying cultural norms. However, students "were not given the opportunity to challenge [local] expectations or to think critically about the cultural biases they perpetuated."[22] This critical awareness is essential both for thinking about our own stories but also for the ability to listen carefully and thoughtfully to others. Todd Snyder's recent work explores the varied ways in which critical pedagogy could benefit students in Appalachia; he cites an example from one of his own classes in which students critiqued stereotypes of Appalachian identity in films, photos, and television shows, and from that "came discussions of class, race, gender, and sexuality." In other words, students were able to start from aspects of their own identities and extend those concepts outward to find commonality with "the marginalization of other social, racial, and ethnic groups in the United States."[23] This kind of critical thinking can help guide us along the threads connecting individuals to communities, communities to cultural or ethnic groups, and cultural or ethnic groups to one another.

———

Another project I test-drove in my community college teaching was not so much a separate project as it was a reworking of an old one: the portfolio. While I was limited in terms of what kinds of essays I could assign (students in this program were required to write separate narrative, definition, and process analysis essays), I localized the focus of these assignments. Students wrote narratives about formative experiences they have had and the influence place had on creating those experiences, such as events with family, learning to swim in local streams or community pools, racing bikes on backyard dirt tracks. They defined concepts, ideas, or terms and considered how their cultural backgrounds have helped shape these definitions. They described things they could do because they had learned them locally—or, they interviewed people who could do local activities that interested them, like canning tomatoes, building hunting bows, or working in community organizations. The types of stories, definitions, and activities students chose would of course have been different in different places; not all parts of Appalachia are the same, after all, and the results I received from my students were focused deeply in the traditions and events of this particular rural region. However, my concern was not so much the specific things they chose to write about, but that they had the experience of thinking and writing about the stories, ideas, and activities they believed were important.

The biggest alteration I made in my approach to the course was in the conception of the final portfolio. I told them to think about the portfolio as an "heirloom collection." "Think of the papers you write this term as something your grandkids'll read one day," I told them. With this in mind, I found that many of my students made additions to the final project I hadn't requested. Some "heirloom collections" came to me with family photos stuffed between essays. Instead of addressing the collection's final reflective letter to me, several addressed it to their future grandchildren. Memorably, one student included in the pocket of her collection's folder a little plastic baggy filled with dust; "That's dirt from the homeplace," she explained to me. Dirt itself, in the stories of who we are, is rhetorical.

What I am saying, in explaining both the history of projects like Foxfire and my own curricular adaptations, is that when place and its influence on our identities becomes part of the educational experience, students can see the value of school in a new way. It can become part of their identities and communities rather than separated from these. I tacked to my office bulletin board a card that the students in one class signed for me at the end of term. "This class wasn't about school, it was about life!" one of them wrote. Lives, I fervently hope, in which writing can mean something more than alienation and abstraction.

Let me be clear: what I am advocating is that Appalachian rhetoric, in all its complex aspects, be brought into the classroom, particularly the writing classroom. Students in such classrooms can investigate their languages, their communication values, and cultures, and they can do it *without losing access to instruction in standard written English and styles of academic writing*. This is a point worth emphasizing. In her influential essay "The Politics of Teaching Literate Discourse," Lisa Delpit made a powerful statement about the absence of standard English, the language of power, in classrooms, particularly for AAVE-speakers and other marginalized students. She pointed out that teachers who focused only on students' home discourses, despite doing so in an attempt to show respect for these discourses, in fact robbed students of the chance to participate in economic and social realms where standardized norms were considered essential. This is a concern that has relevance for people in Appalachia, as well; Elsie Clapp's Arthurdale school suffered from parental concerns that their children weren't learning about how to survive outside the region as well as within it.[24] Yet this is not a problem without a solution; rhetorical education need not be an either/or. Other scholars have demonstrated the educational value of comparative rhetoric in allowing students to experience and understand both the possibilities in their own and other forms of language and rhetoric. Helen Fox examines this issue with regard to international students, demonstrating how the surfacing of different cultures' rhetorical features not only makes them easier to learn, but also helps students to inhabit these features as writers temporarily, without feeling they need betray or disavow their identities in order to do so. Other educators have demonstrated that making vernacular rhetoric and identity part of the classroom can also help students to see the limits of standard English as a language of power. Deborah Sanchez and Eric Paulson cite the work of June Jordan, whose African American students collectively composed a letter protesting police brutality. Her students chose to write their letter in AAVE/Black English:

> They knew that their voices would not be heard, but they chose to write in Black English anyway, to honor the young man who had been killed. With Jordan's help, the students discovered how language is connected with social reality and issues of justice, and they were conscious of their rhetorical choices available.[25]

In other words, these students were able to make a conscious rhetorical choice: their purpose—in this instance, the creation of identity and solidarity—was better served by the use of vernacular rather than standardized language.

Amy D. Clark has likewise argued the multiple values of local and academic literacies for Appalachian peoples. Clark conducted a study of multiple generations of Appalachian women and demonstrated that they were "constantly transmitting or teaching multiple literacies across generations" by using "vernacular literacy practices or those rooted in the everyday activities of home and community."[26] In bringing the ways these literacies work and how this transmitting happens to the surface, Clark likewise argues that Appalachian women can better learn to negotiate new literacies and become more comfortable with themselves as writers, readers, and users of rhetoric. This comfort and flexibility is ultimately something I too, as an Appalachian, want from writing instruction.

Why does it matter if Appalachian students feel alienated from the writing classroom or even education writ large? It matters because the repercussions of that alienation can extend far beyond the schoolroom and even the community. In the final chapter, I will examine the wider relevance of examining Appalachian rhetoric(s), socially and politically.

CHAPTER 9

Rhetoric and Repercussions

The ability to connect students' home and school lives is perhaps most visible in how teachers approach non-standard and marginalized languages. As noted in the last chapter, Lisa Delpit argues for the possibility and necessity of teaching the dominant discourse to students from non-dominant backgrounds. As with Ruby Payne, Delpit's vision of dominant discourse teaching is framed as a moral imperative, as it is through the standard discourse that students can access power. In other words, it is through learning the dominant discourse that students can find pathways to mainstream economic and social success. However, unlike Payne, Delpit specifies that this is not the same thing as eliminating their home dialects; the goal should be, rather, "to add other voices and Discourses to [students'] repertoires."[1] From my experience, Delpit's latter point is being too underplayed in Appalachia. Too often, home dialects aren't conceptualized as *being* home dialects; instead they are conceived of, by students as much as teachers, as ignorance or incorrectness. In much of my educational experience, particularly before I started college, I experienced the privileging of standardized discourse—as language, rhetoric, and identity—without a role or recognition for my home discourse inside the classroom. Reconceiving the goal of rhetorical and writing education away from standardization and to rhetorical sovereignty can allow for equal consideration of the affordances of multiple discourses (including the standard) in the classroom and can bring our schooling experience closer to one of liberation rather than subordination.

Of course, this move would require a concurrent reassessment of societal definitions of success. Right now, educational and social success in the US are deeply entwined with economic gain and claiming middle-class identity. But Appalachian scholars like Todd Snyder are asking us to rethink what the "success" that education provides can mean. As he states, "When Appalachian students begin to question the lessons they learn about themselves both inside and outside the walls of academia, amazing transformations can take place."[2] Those "transformations" don't just mean achieving a low-level technical job. They can mean, as it did for me, a discovery of myself as a writer, as someone capable of critical thought. I want us all to have the chance to think about how we write and speak and why, for ourselves as individuals but also for what we create when we see ourselves as connected. For a long time now I have been, as Sherman Alexie puts it, "writing to save my life."[3] As I have come to see that my life, my voice, are so much more than just myself—it is my family, my roots, the land itself—I have come to see how such writing can be about saving *our* lives, too.

Joel Spring describes what he calls the Pan-Indian movement in the United States; he defines it as a movement that was "based on the assumption that Native American tribes shared a common set of values and interests"[4] and that encouraged strategic consolidations across differences to address social and educational grievances. The movement has succeeded in attaining some improved recognition and legislation in service of greater Native American self-determination, educationally and culturally. (Though you only need to look at the way the water protectors at Standing Rock were treated to see how far away this country's treatment of Native Americans is from being *just*.) I think it is worth considering how this indicates a new potential definition for "success": that success can mean something different than the attainment of middle-class identity. It could mean attaining a sense of faith in one's voice and understanding of how that voice correlates with others. What could Appalachian rhetorical sovereignty offer us that standardization alone does not? Perhaps a better chance at determining our own voices and identities, of claiming a role in the educational curricula and even laws that affect our lives.

———

Appalachia is not simple. That is one of the stereotypes that has done this region the most harm: that Appalachians are simple folk, living simple lives in a simple place. I tend to think the opposite is true, that due to its sheer expanse of territory, in- and out-migration, the diversity of peoples, and multiplicity of social influences, Appalachia is more culturally complex than many regions of the world. We are eternally what Gloria Anzaldua describes as a border region, where discourses meet, mix, and sometimes clash. What I have tried to do here is trace one thread, one tradition, one influence shaping the ways Appalachian peoples may create and communicate identity. I don't claim that this is the only thread, the only tradition, or the only influence. I have foregrounded a form of non-adversarial argument common in the writings of Appalachian authors, which I perceive as rooted in a regional geography and cultural history. However, this is not the only way in which Appalachian people compose arguments. I have purposely, up until now, avoided the *very* adversarial argument tradition that Appalachia is stereotyped with, that of the feud. A recent resurgence of interest in the Hatfields and McCoys has ensured that new correlations will continue to be drawn between Appalachian culture and predilections for violence, correlations that might seem at odds with my description of a non-adversarial argument tradition. When I described Appalachian non-adversarial argument to my office-mate Lisa, she nodded thoughtfully. "It makes sense," she said. "There's probably a cultural hesitance to cause offense, because feuds can last for so long."

From a cultural standpoint, she might be onto something. When having deep family loyalty and a long memory is seen as a social value, the potential for lingering and explosive resentments can be enduring. I've also seen some rip-roaring arguments take place in my family, without a lick of "non-adversarial" about them. But I think it's noteworthy that those arguments happened *within the family.* There's a sense of safety, a loosening of the rules of interaction, when we can be reasonably sure that the people we're fighting with will forgive our offenses. Outside the family circle, preserving lines of connection is perhaps a more tenuous proposition, one that needs to be cultivated carefully.

Ultimately, while my points about the nature and history of Appalachian rhetoric may not be as easily generalizable as they initially appear, I hope they can be a starting point. As I said, I want other Appalachian students and teachers, whether they were born here or not, to consider these issues for themselves. I want them to consider further how building and linking our Appalachian identities (whether or not those identities end up looking the same) can help us make demands for the educational, aesthetic, and legal well-being of ourselves, our families, and our lands. I want us to understand our own rhetorics, how we can use them, and how we can see when they are being used against us.

———

In 2014, *New Yorker* staff writer Jeffrey Toobin published a piece titled "What's the Matter with West Virginia?" Judging by the title alone, I was afraid I would encounter yet another "what's wrong with these people" description of Appalachian backwardness. What I found instead was a meditation on a question that does seem to be quite perplexing. Toobin can't understand why West Virginians continue to offer tacit support to the industry leaders and right-wing politicians that seem willing, if not eager, to do harm to the state's land and people. He specifies the case of Massey Energy executive Don Blankenship, who "engaged in a lengthy pattern of deception in dealings with federal mine regulators, in an effort to cut costs, and, consequently, exposed his employees to appalling risks" (including the 2010 disaster at Upper Big Branch, where twenty-nine miners died). Yet the state continues to elect, by huge margins, the Republican politicians supported by firms like Massey Energy, who campaign on promises to fight *against* regulations and EPA efforts to protect land, air, and water from harmful extractive industry practices. I, too, find this pattern troubling and deeply frustrating. Appalachian culture, as I have experienced it and according to every source I've read about it, is a culture that values place. (Recall that oil man's exasperation that people wouldn't just leave their land when it became polluted.) In fact, I have never talked to a person from this region who gave me the indication that they didn't care about the land. Why then does West Virginia, and other parts of Appalachia, continue to support people who don't?

Toobin wonders if the disconnect is, in fact, one of rhetoric. As he notes, "It's a good bet that a majority of the Massey miners, whose lives Blankenship may have placed in jeopardy and whom the federal bureaucrats [under the Obama administration] were trying to protect, voted Republican," largely on the basis of perception. He concludes that Democratic politicians in West Virginia are regarded as "an alien force," outsider elitists whose goal is to dominate rather than cooperate. What Toobin wants is for Democratic politicians to *learn to talk to West Virginians*. The inference, then, is that Republicans already know how to do this. Industrialists like Blankenship and the politicians he supports have learned to convey themselves, to West Virginians, as "one of you," a status that can cover a vast amount of sins. Is it, in fact, the ethos rather than the ideas that are being elected, and do the voters realize *why* they find that ethos so trustworthy? Even when that trust, as in the case of Don Blankenship, is so grossly misplaced?

Toobin wants those losing Democratic politicians to, essentially, learn a new rhetoric. I wonder, though, what might happen if more of West Virginia's voters had access to a comprehensive rhetorical education, as well. I don't mean, as I think Toobin does, that I simply want Appalachians to stop voting Republican and start voting Democrat. What I want is to be sure more of us understand when we're being rhetorically played, and how, and what that means for what we in fact really care about and want to see in the world. It seems to me that the story we are so often told, by the extractive industries, media, and even the schools, is that those politicians who "get" us have our best interests at heart. Too few seem to look beyond that, to evaluate closely what those interests, both the politicians' and our own, actually are.

I have been contending that Appalachians have the right to speak and be heard, but I also attest that we deserve the right to educations that help us critique the stories we tell and are told. It would help if, first, we had a chance to think about what our rhetoric *is*, what it indicates, and how it can be used for, or against, our interests. It seems more important than ever now, when Donald Trump swept the vote in most Appalachian states on the basis of a lie: he would bring back coal jobs.

It's hard to understand why so many Appalachians reacted to Hilary Clinton with hostility, especially given that she presented a realistic plan for reinvigorating our economies: renewable energy. Why on earth would so many people cling so religiously to an industry that has brought us and our land so much death and destruction? It is a question I cannot truly claim to answer myself. Is there anything Clinton, a woman and a career Democratic politician, could have said that would have swayed those voters? All I know is what I would have said were I in her position. I would have told them about my great-grandfather, who mined coal to keep his family fed and clothed. I would have shown them the picture, one of the oldest we have in my family, of him standing outside a coal shack, arms crossed, pride in every muscle of his frame. Then I would have told them about his son, my grandfather, who fought and nearly died in World War II. He lost an arm in Germany, which when he returned took coal mining out of the running as a career, but he knew technology and learned to repair televisions. He traveled across three counties fixing TVs, back before people threw away anything that stopped working, and he was remembered fondly for it all his life. I would tell them that my grandfather wasted nothing. We still have a shed filled with his old stockpile of television parts that he wouldn't throw away, just in case he needed them. He grew nearly everything his family ate; at his peak, that included managing upwards of five gardens and veritable orchards of fruit trees and berry vines in three different yards. During the season, he went out to the woods to collect walnuts, hickory nuts, and pawpaws. If he could have powered his home with the sun and wind, he would have done it *in a heartbeat*. To waste the sunshine and air that we have is to insult those hardworking men and women who came before us, who knew the value of using what you had. Use it up, wear it out, make it do, or do without. Instead, we keep forcing our way into the mountains God put there, putting money, energy, our land's health, and our own lives at stake to mine coal, ignoring the resources that are readily available to us. If we keep wasting those renewable resources—sun and wind that could be powering our homes and the nation without destroying our land and our health—then by God I think that we *deserve* to do without.

That's what I think, anyway. You can think what you want.

———

In 2011, Marilyn M. Cooper published the article "Rhetorical Agency as Emergent and Enacted" in *CCC*. In her piece, Cooper came to the following conclusion:

> What we need is not a pedagogy of empowerment, but a pedagogy of responsibility. We need to help students understand that writing and speaking (rhetoric) are always serious actions. The meanings they create in their rhetoric arise from and feed back into the construction of their own dispositions, their own ethos. What they write or argue, as with all other actions they perform, makes them who they are.[5]

When we compose, we compose ourselves, and not just for others. I think of those Appalachian memoirs, which seemed so aware of that concept. They were composing themselves; specifically, they were composing their lives in places, and were inviting others, readers, to witness that composition. Even before this book had begun to take shape in my mind and through my hands, back when I first read Cooper's article for a course on rhetorical theory, I made a note in the margin. "This idea sounds very Appalachian," I had written. Wouldn't it be something if, for once, we could be seen as being on the intellectual cutting edge.

———

In her book *Storytelling for Social Justice*, Lee Anne Bell demonstrates how stories can become stock narratives—the ideas we repeat so often to ourselves that we forget to question them.[6] They are stories that support the status quo, keeping power dynamics between races, genders, and economic classes fundamentally uneven. Yet, our stories are also some of the best ways by which to question these narratives, if we can learn to listen critically to what those stories say and how our context influences us as audiences. In other words, we need to think carefully about who gets to speak and who has to listen (or not). Because the listening, not just the speaking, can mean a great deal for how we think of ourselves and others. Herbert Roth describes how, between 1935 and 1937, his village in Germany turned against its Jewish inhabitants, including himself: through silence and indifference.[7] Very quickly, Jewish peoples lost the right to speak and non-Jewish Germans the responsibility to listen. The result was a complete change in who was considered valuable, worthwhile, even human.

Because speaking and listening to stories are acts of such power, acts that can potentially convey or deny power to others, I treat them with great care. One of Emmy's Christmas presents was a video dance game for the Nintendo that we keep down home ("down home" being my grandparents' house; the trailer a little further up the hill where I grew up, and where Emmy lived until the trailer was replaced by a double-wide, has long been known as "up home"). Not long ago, I was playing this game with Emmy and one of her friends. After a few random song selections, the two of them chose to dance to a song that recently overtook popular radio, despite having lyrics promoting rape and violence against women.

"Not that 'un," I immediately said, forgetting for the moment that such an approach is never successful with children, unless one has the parental authority to back it up. Both girls knew perfectly well I did not.

"Fine," I said, after unsuccessful haggling, "you two go right ahead, but I ain't playing until that song is over."

"Why not?" Emmy asked, clearly confused. I gave her a quick hug while I headed out of the room, to show her that I wasn't acting from anger. "It's a song about hurting people, and I don't care to hear it again," I said, and left. She and her friend danced to the song, then called me back. And they didn't pick that song again. I'll take that as a win.

But what did I win? I've thought about this a good deal since. In retrospect, I'm glad I didn't succeed in dissuading them from the song altogether—I don't want to discourage the importance of listening in order to critique. Without knowing what the song said, how could one carefully think about the message it conveys? Emmy is thoughtful; I think it likely she has considered it. But whether she has or not, I think about what it is she saw in that moment. I didn't, ultimately, refuse them a song that troubled me. I didn't deny the singer his right to sing what he wants. But I also didn't accept it. I spoke my piece: I didn't participate in the dehumanization of women by virtue of silence. What I hope Emmy saw is that even the songs we listen to have influence; they can shape us, but we can also choose how we want to be shaped and why. Hear it out, think about it, and decide what you want. Rhetoric is not only how we persuade other people. It's how we are persuaded, built, created by others. I refused to allow that text to create me, to shape what I think of as normal and expected. I rejected it for myself. I hope Emmy will learn to pay attention to texts, to decide for herself what she wants to let in, to stitch together into an identity for herself, to quilt into her own life.

When discussing her book of Appalachian story-poems *Kettlebottom*, Diane Gilliam Fisher made the point that "Stories are how people get to be who they are." They are certainly how I've gotten to be me. If I argue anything in a traditional academic sense, let it be that stories, rhetorics, are how Appalachia has come to be what it is, even if those stories don't end up where you'd expect them to, or maybe don't end at all. Like Todd Snyder said, some of us kind of like our stories that way. It is the process of coming to be that matters. It is the glorious array of colors that make the quilt what it is, and the choices of those colors that make it ours.

———

When I began this project, I was raw with the fear that my family would be broken apart, that Emmy and David would be taken from us by a court system that privileged their non-Appalachian father. I felt silenced by that system because it couldn't understand my role in their lives or their role in mine. And in the last month of writing this text, I lost my grandfather, my Pap, the last grandparent I had. I find myself overwhelmed by the weight of stories I'll never hear and terror that I'll forget the ones I have heard. What I find is that I feel more urgency now, more responsibility than I felt even when I began, to say something that will give back to the culture that made him and that made me. Far from being made less by our Appalachian-ness, as deficit ideology says we are, I feel I owe something to it, for giving me these people, these places, these stories. This quilt, then, is what I have to give.

I began with the premise that there is something real to being Appalachian, in the sense that it has influenced my ways of thinking, acting, and valuing. However, these differences can be, and too often are being, framed as deficits, or overlooked completely, in the academic arenas more Appalachian students are finding themselves in. I raised the possibility of considering Appalachia in terms of rhetorical sovereignty, as defined by Scott Richard Lyons: "a people's control of its meaning."[8] Composition studies, Lyons argues, can help peoples achieve this control through helping students from non-dominant cultures critique rhetorical imperialism and determine their own communicative needs. Rhetorical sovereignty, when it exists, can have social, legal, and educational repercussions; without it, Appalachia is that much easier to dismiss as culturally invalid or irrelevant. However, what makes rhetorical sovereignty difficult to apply to Appalachia specifically is the concept's definition of what makes a group into a people: "human beings united together by history, language, culture, or some combination therein."[9] Appalachia can, and has, been defined as a wide geographical expanse, a range that crosses multiple state boundaries. Can the inhabitants of this expanse be considered a "people" in a way that would allow us to campaign for our own rhetorical sovereignty, the right to claim our own definitions, and have them respected?

My sense, and what I've attempted to work through in this writing, is yes, though in complicated ways, ways we likely cannot begin to conceptualize in isolation. It is an answer predicated on a potentially uniting thread: Appalachian narrative rhetoric, with its forms, history, and epistemology, can strategically link us together and set us apart from the academic mainstream. I've attempted, in chapter three, to root this rhetoric historically as an influence from early Scotch-Irish homesteaders, who brought with them a rhetorical system based not on classical forms but on Celtic ones. For emigrants from Europe's Celtic Fringe, the influence of the Greco-Roman world would have been historically less prominent, whereas Celtic rhetoric had developed over centuries to fit the social and physical geographies of the Celtic countries. I sought ways of defining and analyzing Celtic rhetoric; the result, while likely simplistic, I posit to be nonetheless worthwhile as a potential starting point for analyzing the rhetorics of Appalachia, particularly as they appear in writing. Chapters four and five expand on this; I hoped to show what a written Appalachian rhetoric can look like and why it takes the forms it does. These, for me, are essential concepts if this form of Appalachian rhetoric is ever to have a hearing in rhetoric and composition classrooms, or beyond. If the classroom is ever to become a space through which we as Appalachian students can start to see ourselves as a linked people, and beyond this, to critique rhetorical imperialism and determine our own communicative needs, there must be an acknowledgment that we have something to be respected for and to contribute to those classrooms.

Whether or not we find a space in schools for Appalachian rhetoric and rhetorical sovereignty may rely on the views of the non-Appalachian, mainstream decision-makers who determine curriculum. Lyons's rhetorical sovereignty has two interlinked components: it is the right of a people to define their own meaning, but it is also the willingness of others to respect that definition. It is the latter consideration that determined my later chapters. What inhibits us, in other words, from being seen from the outside as having culture or rhetoric, as opposed to simply being educationally underprepared and in need of standardization? The answer might have something to do with a failure to see Appalachia as historically and culturally influenced in ways distinct from non-Appalachian regions of the country—with seeing Appalachia as fundamentally white, Anglo-Saxon, and Protestant in the same ways the American elite. Steamrolling cultural or rhetorical difference, and establishing the defining feature of Appalachian identity as poverty, allows for simplistic notions of education and success for Appalachian students. What we "need," in this view, is standardization, which ideally allows us to gain quasi-lucrative jobs and middle-class social identities. In this system, skill-and-drill standardization becomes not only the central feature of the classroom, it also becomes a moral imperative for teachers seeking to improve the quality of students' lives. What goes unseen is what stands to be lost by such "improvement," the potential stakes implicit in cultural denigration.

These final chapters are the most difficult for me to write or even to conceive. They make me feel the most like I'm writing in the dark. I've tried to explain what I want to see happen in our classrooms, to provide guidance or ideas for alternatives that avoid cultural denigration, and that offer steps toward Appalachian rhetorical sovereignty. These are the most difficult for me because, ultimately, I don't know what will work and what won't. That will require both time and concerted effort on the parts of many more people than just me. My hope is not, then, that educators will attempt to follow my pedagogical suggestions verbatim, but rather that they will start to ask their Appalachian students to think about their identities and rhetorical desires and how to make these known. Who knows what we will learn, about ourselves and about each other?

———

When I was about eleven or twelve years old, I got very interested in herbal medicines. A lot of this had to do with knowing I had a family connection to midwives and root doctors like my three-times great-grandmother Granny Elizabeth. I also liked the idea of using what we could from the land.

Pap took me into the woods to show me where a patch of goldenseal grew. Goldenseal was precious; while it didn't fetch as high a price as ginseng, you could still be certain that if too many people knew it was here, we would come back one day to find it all dug up and hauled away. I don't know, now that I think of it, if this patch was one that Pap planted or that happened to crop up on its own. Goldenseal is notoriously hard to grow, but I imagine he would have had the patience to do it. (He tended to have far more patience with plants than with people.) He showed me how to dig up some of the bright yellow root, but told me to always leave as much of it in the ground as I could, so it would sprout again. *Don't waste anything*, was the subtext. Especially something as special as goldenseal.

Different people have different ideas about what exactly goldenseal can treat. Pap used it for mouth sores and overall oral health. One harvest could last a good long while; you just let the roots dry, then chewed on a tiny, bitter nip when needed. I didn't think about the goldenseal patch for years after, until in the last year of his life Pap developed a bad sore but didn't have any goldenseal on hand. I went to find the patch again . . . and couldn't. The path was entirely overgrown, and even when I did manage to make my way through briars and tree limbs to where I'd thought it was, the ground was overrun with may apple, a plant that superficially resembles goldenseal, with the difference of being toxic to ingest. I looked and looked and became more despairing with every step. I had failed to remember what he had told me, just when I needed to remember it the most.

———

When I was an undergrad, I said in a paper that I liked good questions because there was always the chance that they'd have good answers. Maybe all I've done over these pages is raise questions, hopefully good ones. But the best one I find myself faced with now is one that I think Lyons would advocate: *What do I, as an Appalachian, want from writing instruction?* I want it to help me record and remember my stories and to hear new ones; I want it to respect my stories and to help me mine them for meaning, then share them the best ways I can. I want it to help me see why family and place seem to stand for the same things in my mind and why I look to these as a means by which to create knowledge. I want it to help me create that knowledge. And I want it to help me tell the world who I am, who we are, and to claim the world's respect.

Are these good answers? I don't know yet. I want to hear a lot more first, then maybe I can decide.

A few years ago, I crocheted lap blankets for each of my grandparents. Pap in particular always hated the cold and would turn the heat up so high that the rest of us would actually step outside into the winter cold to get a few minutes' relief. If you've had much experience with crochet, you know that it can have a lace-like appearance; Pap took one look at my gift and frowned. "How's that s'posed to keep you warm? It's got holes in it." No doubt he would have preferred a quilt. I found out later, though, that he told my mother, "You know, that blanket really is purty warm." I put it in the casket when we buried him; I couldn't bear to see it on the bed by itself. If I was a quilter, maybe I could've found a way to sew part of it into a new blanket. But my quilting uses a keyboard rather than cloth, so I didn't need Pap's blanket. He'd given me stories instead.

The blanket I crocheted had holes. The colors of Alty's quilt clashed. Ain't none of us can satisfy everyone. It's hard enough to satisfy ourselves. The least we can have is the chance to try.

Notes

INTRODUCTION: WRITING TAKES PLACE

1. Hofstra, *Ulster to America: The Scots-Irish Migration Experience, 1680–1830*, xvii.
2. Clark, "Letters from Home," 64.
3. Lyons, "Rhetorical Sovereignty," 462.

1. ETHOS

1. Trask, *From a Native Daughter*, quoted in Lyons, "Rhetorical Sovereignty," 462.
2. Williams, *The Alchemy of Race and Rights*, 48.
3. "The Appalachian Region," *Appalachian Regional Commission*.
4. "The Appalachian Region," *Appalachian Regional Commission*.
5. "About ARC," *Appalachian Regional Commission*.
6. Dallas, "'Hillbilly Elegy': Best-selling author."
7. Green, "It Was Cultural Anxiety."
8. Lyons, "Rhetorical Sovereignty," 449–50.
9. Lyons, "Rhetorical Sovereignty," 454.
10. Villanueva, foreword to *Whistlin' and Crowin*,' xv.
11. Lyons, "Rhetorical Sovereignty," 462.
12. Trask, *From a Native Daughter*, quoted in Lyons, "Rhetorical Sovereignty," 462.

2. LANGUAGE

1. Fleckenstein et al., "The Importance of Harmony," 393.
2. Iddings and Angus, "A Functional Linguistics," 168.
3. Smitherman, *Talkin that Talk*, 19.
4. Payne, *A Framework for Understanding Poverty*, 10.
5. "Banned Terms," email message to author.
6. This project also ignored some of the best practices in the educational field. For example, Rebecca Wheeler and Rachel Swords, authors of *Codeswitching: Tools of Language and Culture Transform the Dialectally Diverse Classroom*, have demonstrated great success using contrastive analysis in their work with AAVE-speaking students in Virginia. Through contrastive

analysis, students are able to recognize and compare the grammatical features of both their home dialects and standardized English without presenting either as inherently more correct.

7. Cited in Elbow, "Inviting the Mother Tongue," 359.
8. Montgomery, "How Scotch-Irish Is Your English?"
9. Jackson, "Peoples of Appalachia," 27.
10. Thompson and Moser, "Appalachian Folklife," 147–50.
11. Montgomery, "The Historical Background and Nature of the Englishes of Appalachia," 25.
12. Jackson, "Peoples of Appalachia," 35.
13. Lyons, "Rhetorical Sovereignty," 454.
14. Horner and Trimbur, "English Only and U.S. College Composition."
15. Adams, "Little Betty and Amos (Live)."
16. Donehower, "Rhetorics and Realities," 49.
17. Montgomery, "How Scotch-Irish Is Your English?"
18. Montgomery, "Language," 1003.
19. *Mountain Talk.*
20. William Wallace is the historical Scottish warrior portrayed in the film *Braveheart.*
21. Smith, "Southern Exposure," 205.
22. Montgomery, "How Scotch-Irish Is Your English?"
23. Montgomery, "The Historical Background and Nature of the Englishes of Appalachia," 35.
24. Reaser, "Dialect and Education in Appalachia," 104–106.
25. Clark, "Voices in the Appalachian Classroom," 110.

3. CELTIC RHETORIC

1. Anderson, "Ethnography, Stance, and Appalachian Migrants in Detroit."
2. Hutton, "Hillbilly Elitism."
3. Brown, Hirschman, and Maclaran, *Two Continents, One Culture,* vii.
4. O' Snodaigh, *Hidden Ulster,* 29.
5. Brown, Hirschman, and Maclaran, *Two Continents, One Culture,* 3.
6. Hofstra, *Ulster to America,* 11.
7. Brown, Hirschman, and Maclaran. *Two Continents, One Culture,* 5.
8. Pryce, *Literacy in Medieval Celtic Societies,* 2–3.
9. Fulton, *Medieval Celtic Literature and Society,* 11.
10. O' Snodaigh, *Hidden Ulster,* 29–33.
11. Jackson, "Peoples of Appalachia," 35.
12. Lynch, "'Ego Patricius,'" 116.
13. O'Riordan, *The Gaelic Mind;* Marshall, *Nature's Web;* Scherman, *The Flowering of Ireland.*
14. O'Riordan, *The Gaelic Mind;* Stacey, "Law and Literature"; N. Patterson, *Cattle Lords and Clansmen.*

15. Lynch, "'Ego Patricius'"; Connell, "Writing on the Land of Ireland."

16. Lynch, "'Ego Patricius'"; O'Riordan, *The Gaelic Mind*; Connell, "Writing on the Land of Ireland"; Johnson-Sheehan and Lynch, "Rhetoric of Myth, Magic, and Conversion."

17. Marshall, *Nature's Web*, 90.

18. McCrumb, *Sharyn McCrumb's Appalachia*, 50.

19. O' Riordan, *The Gaelic Mind*, 1.

20. Johnson-Sheehan and Lynch, "Rhetoric of Myth, Magic, and Conversion," 243.

21. Berry, *The Unsettling of America*, 19.

22. O' Driscoll, *The Celtic Consciousness*, 200.

23. Johnson-Sheehan and Lynch, "Rhetoric of Myth, Magic, and Conversion," 244.

24. Bizzell and Herzberg, General Introduction to *The Rhetorical Tradition*, 1–2.

25. Lynch, "'Ego Patricius,'" 114.

26. O' Driscoll, *The Celtic Consciousness*, xiv.

27. Lynch, "'Ego Patricius,'" 115.

28. O' Riordan, *The Gaelic Mind*, 4.

29. Johnson-Sheehan and Lynch, "Rhetoric of Myth, Magic, and Conversion," 242.

30. Lynch, "'Ego Patricius,'" 116.

31. O' Riordan, *The Gaelic Mind*, 7.

32. Patterson, *Cattle Lords and Clansmen*, 8.

33. Stacey, "Law and Literature in Medieval Ireland and Wales," 65–69.

34. Stacey, "Law and Literature in Medieval Ireland and Wales," 75.

35. Connell, "Writing on the Land of Ireland."

36. *The Hunger Games*, a novel by Suzanne Collins turned hit film, is set in a dystopic future where teenagers from each region or "district" of what was once the USA must fight to the death for the entertainment of the elite. The main character, Katniss, is one of her district's "tributes" in the games, representing District 12: Appalachia.

37. Donehower, "Rhetorics and Realities," 44.

38. Jones, *Appalachian Values*, 51.

39. Fulton, *Medieval Celtic Literature and Society*, 14.

40. Hofstra, *Ulster to America*, xvii.

41. Sohn, *Whistlin' and Crowin' Women of Appalachia*, 1.

4. CELTIC RHETORIC IN APPALACHIA

1. Locklear, "Narrating Socialization," 41–43.

2. Sohn, *Whistlin' and Crowin' Women of Appalachia*, 18.

3. Sohn, "Silence, Voice, and Identity among Appalachian College Women," 126.

4.   Sohn, *Whistlin' and Crowin' Women of Appalachia*, 36.
5.   Sohn, "Silence, Voice, and Identity among Appalachian College Women," 129.
6.   Shepley, "Places of Composition," 85.
7.   Joyce, "A Woman's Place," 20.
8.   Lynn, *Coal Miner's Daughter*, xiv.
9.   Shepley, "Places of Composition," 83.
10. Shepley, "Places of Composition," 83.
11. Shepley, "Places of Composition," 84.
12. O' Driscoll, *The Celtic Consciousness*, 289.
13. Johnson-Sheehan and Lynch, "Rhetoric of Myth, Magic, and Conversion," 234–36.
14. Holloway, *From a Race of Storytellers*, 180.
15. McCrumb, *The Songcatcher*, 309.
16. Pryce, *Literacy in Medieval Celtic Societies*, 11.
17. Corbett and Connors, *Classical Rhetoric for the Modern Student*, 1.
18. Bullock, *The Norton Field Guide to Writing*, 97.
19. DiYanni and Hoy, II, *Frames of Mind*, 614.
20. Ritchie and Ronald, *Available Means*, xx.

5. WRITING AN APPALACHIAN RHETORIC

1.   Connell, "Writing on the Land of Ireland."
2.   Connell, "Writing on the Land of Ireland."
3.   Connell, "Writing on the Land of Ireland."
4.   Kindness, *The Way It Was*, 30.
5.   Connell, "Writing on the Land of Ireland."
6.   Kindness, *The Way It Was*, 30–31.
7.   Kindness, *The Way It Was*, 30.
8.   Harper, *An Enchanted Childhood at Raven Rocks*, 1.
9.   Harper, *An Enchanted Childhood at Raven Rocks*, 8.
10. Kindness, *The Way It Was*, 1.
11. Harper, *An Enchanted Childhood at Raven Rocks*, 1.
12. Harper, *An Enchanted Childhood at Raven Rocks*, 223.
13. Harper, *An Enchanted Childhood at Raven Rocks*, 223.
14. Lynch, "'Ego Patricius,'" 116.
15. Harper, *An Enchanted Childhood at Raven Rocks*, 2.
16. Harper, *An Enchanted Childhood at Raven Rocks*, 14.
17. Stacey, "Law and Literature in Medieval Ireland and Wales," 75.
18. Harper, *An Enchanted Childhood at Raven Rocks*, 5.
19. Harper, *An Enchanted Childhood at Raven Rocks*, 8–9.
20. Kindness, *The Way It Was*, 2.
21. Kindness, *The Way It Was*, 2.
22. Elbow, "Bringing the Rhetoric of Assent and the Believing Game Together," 397.

23. Elbow, "Bringing the Rhetoric of Assent and the Believing Game Together," 397.
24. Harper, *An Enchanted Childhood at Raven Rocks*, 224.
25. Harper, *An Enchanted Childhood at Raven Rocks*, 13.
26. Harper, *An Enchanted Childhood at Raven Rocks*, 14.
27. Harper, *An Enchanted Childhood at Raven Rocks*, 223.
28. Harper, *An Enchanted Childhood at Raven Rocks*, 224.
29. Harper, *An Enchanted Childhood at Raven Rocks*, 45.
30. Harper, *An Enchanted Childhood at Raven Rocks*, 45.
31. Clark, "Letters from Home," 64.
32. Clark, "Letters from Home," 54.
33. Lynch, "'Ego Patricius,'" 115.

6. WHEN RHETORIC IS A DEFICIT

1. Gee, "Literacy, Discourse, and Linguistics," 7.
2. Sohn, *Whistlin' and Crowin' Women of Appalachia*, 71.
3. Snyder, *The Rhetoric of Appalachian Identity*, 71.
4. Satlin and Levine, "White House Budget Director Says Single Moms Shouldn't Have to Pay for PBS."
5. Lewis, "The Colony of Appalachia," 2.
6. Monique Redeaux notes the dangers that can result from law officers imbibing Payne's argument that the poor are "inherently violent" and unable to consider long-term consequences. When one of her own students is killed by a police officer, Redeaux wonders if it was because the officer "looked at Ellis and saw the person Payne describes" (180). Given current events, a reconsideration of Payne's ideology seems timely.
7. Payne, *A Framework for Understanding Poverty*, 37.
8. Payne, *A Framework for Understanding Poverty*, 36.
9. Payne, *A Framework for Understanding Poverty*, 39.
10. Payne, *A Framework for Understanding Poverty*, 79.
11. Payne, *A Framework for Understanding Poverty*, 49.
12. Keown-Bomar and Patee, "What's Class Got to Do with It?," 215.
13. Ahlquist et al., Introduction to *Assault on Kids*, 1.
14. Ahlquist et al., Introduction to *Assault on Kids*, 1.
15. Ahlquist et al., Introduction to *Assault on Kids*, 2.
16. Gorski, "Unlearning Deficit Ideology and the Scornful Gaze," 152–53.
17. Redeaux, "A Framework for Maintaining White Privilege," 194.
18. Ahlquist et al., Introduction to *Assault on Kids*, 4.
19. Montano and Quintanar-Sarellana, "Undoing Ruby Payne," 199.
20. Donehower, "Rhetorics and Realities," 46.
21. On a related note, it's a running joke on the popular sitcom *Big Bang Theory* that the character Penny is described as a "hillbilly" or one of "the hillfolk." Her character, it has been well-established, is from the Great Plains state of Nebraska.

22.   Snyder, *The Rhetoric of Appalachian Identity*, 16–17.
23.   *Appalachian Perspectives at Ohio University: Findings of Spring 2004 Survey*, 1.
24.   Donehower, "Rhetorics and Realities," 49, 39.
25.   Donehower, "Rhetorics and Realities," 41.
26.   Snyder, *The Rhetoric of Appalachian Identity*, 74.
27.   Mathieu et al., *Writing Places*, xv.
28.   McCrumb, *Sharyn McCrumb's Appalachia*, 23–24.
29.   "Bitter Work." *Avatar: The Last Airbender*.
30.   Sohn, *Whistlin' and Crowin' Women of Appalachia*, 1.

7. CATEGORIZING EDUCATION

1.   Donehower, "Rhetorics and Realities," 60.
2.   Eller, quoted in DeWitt, "Historian: Appalachia Has Record of Social Injustice."
3.   Purcell-Gates, "'. . . As Soon As She Opened Her Mouth!,'" 122.
4.   Beech, "Redneck and Hillbilly Discourse," 184.
5.   Heath, *Ways with Words*, 354.
6.   Heath, *Ways with Words*, 343.
7.   Heath, *Ways with Words*, 356.
8.   Heath, *Ways with Words*, 357.
9.   Heath, *Ways with Words*, 359.
10.   "Ohio Social Studies Standards," *Ohio Department of Education*.
11.   Harris, "The Idea of Community in the Study of Writing," 19.
12.   Berry, *The Unsettling of America*, 19.
13.   Berry, *The Unsettling of America*, 19.
14.   Payne, *A Framework for Understanding Poverty*, 49.
15.   Madden, *A Pocketful of Essays*, 7.
16.   Brandon, *At a Glance: Essays*, 55–56.
17.   Madden, *A Pocketful of Essays*, 115.
18.   Brandon, *At a Glance: Essays*, 167–168.
19.   Donehower, "Rhetorics and Realities," 51.
20.   Donehower, "Rhetorics and Realities," 51–52.
21.   Donehower, "Rhetorics and Realities," 54.
22.   Donehower, "Rhetorics and Realities," 53.
23.   Donehower, "Rhetorics and Realities," 51.
24.   Donehower, "Rhetorics and Realities," 51.
25.   Beech, "Redneck and Hillbilly Discourse," 184.
26.   Whited, "Review: The Hunger Games," 327–28.
27.   Collins, *The Hunger Games*, 49.
28.   Jones, *Appalachian Values*, 123.
29.   Lindgren, "Blogging Places: Locating Pedagogy in the Whereness of Weblogs."

8. EDUCATION AND RHETORICAL IDENTITY

1. Valentine, *West Virginia Quilts and Quiltmakers*, 92.
2. Stacey, "Law and Literature in Medieval Ireland and Wales," 75.
3. Kirk and Okazawa-Rey, *Women's Lives*, 565.
4. Kirk and Okazawa-Rey, *Women's Lives*, 566.
5. Snyder, *The Rhetoric of Appalachian Identity*, 16.
6. Lyons, "Rhetorical Sovereignty," 449–50.
7. Penix, *Arthurdale*, 59.
8. Clapp, *Community Schools in Action*, 51.
9. Penix, *Arthurdale*, 59.
10. Heath, *Ways with Words*, 265–66.
11. Heath, *Ways with Words*, 317.
12. Heath, *Ways with Words*, 320.
13. Sohn, *Whistlin' and Crowin' Women of Appalachia*, 77.
14. Heath, *Ways with Words*, 343.
15. Wigginton, "Introduction to *The Foxfire Book*" 12–13.
16. Teets, "Education in Appalachia," 135.
17. Gee, "Literacy, Discourse, and Linguistics: Introduction," 6.
18. Fox, *Listening to the World*, ix.
19. Fox, *Listening to the World*, 10.
20. Fox, *Listening to the World*, xviii.
21. Fox, *Listening to the World*, 108.
22. Azano, "The Possibility of Place," 7–9.
23. Snyder, *The Rhetoric of Appalachian Identity*, 182.
24. Theobald, *Education Now*," 124.
25. Sanchez and Paulson, "Critical Language Awareness," 170.
26. Clark, "Letters from Home," 55.

9. RHETORIC AND REPERCUSSIONS

1. Delpit, "The Politics of Teaching Literate Discourse," 293.
2. Snyder, *The Rhetoric of Appalachian Identity*, 14.
3. Alexie, "The Joy of Reading and Writing: Superman and Me."
4. Spring, *The American School*, 396.
5. Cooper, "Rhetorical Agency as Emergent and Enacted," 443.
6. Bell, *Storytelling for Social Justice*, 29.
7. Roth et al., "An Unlikely Alliance," 59.
8. Lyons, "Rhetorical Sovereignty," 447.
9. Lyons, "Rhetorical Sovereignty," 454.

BIBLIOGRAPHY

"About ARC." *Appalachian Regional Commission.* Accessed August 10, 2014. https://www.arc.gov/about/index.asp.

Adams, Sheila Kay. "Little Betty and Amos (Live)." *Whatever Happened to John Parrish's Boy?* Mars Hill, NC: Granny Dell Records, 2005.

Ahlquist, Roberta, Paul Gorski, and Theresa Montaño. Introduction to *Assault on Kids: How Hyper-Accountability, Corporatization, Deficit Ideologies, and Ruby Payne are Destroying Our Schools,* 1–8. New York: Peter Lang, 2011.

Alexie, Sherman. "The Joy of Reading and Writing: Superman and Me." *Los Angeles Times.* April 19, 1998.

Anderson, Bridget. "Ethnography, Stance, and Appalachian Migrants in Detroit." Presentation at the Appalachian Studies Association Conference, Huntington, WV, March 2014.

Appalachian Perspectives at Ohio University: Findings of Spring 2004 Survey. By the Appalachian Faculty Learning Community. 2005.

"The Appalachian Region." *Appalachian Regional Commission.* Accessed August 10, 2014, https://www.arc.gov/appalachian_region/TheAppalachianRegion.asp.

Awiakta, Marilou. *Selu: Seeking the Corn Mother's Wisdom.* Golden, CO: Fulcrum Publishing, 1993.

Azano, Amy. "The Possibility of Place: One Teacher's Use of Place-Based Instruction for English Students in a Rural High School." *Journal of Research in Rural Education* 26, no. 10 (2011): 1–12.

Beech, Jennifer. "Redneck and Hillbilly Discourse in the Writing Classroom: Classifying Critical Pedagogies of Whiteness." *College English* 67, no. 2 (2004): 172–86.

Bell, Lee Anne. *Storytelling for Social Justice.* New York: Routledge, 2010.

Berry, Wendell. *The Unsettling of America: Culture & Agriculture.* 3rd ed. San Francisco: Sierra Club Books, 1996.

"Bitter Work." *Avatar: The Last Airbender.* Directed by Ethan Spaulding. Burbank, CA: Nickelodeon Animation Studios, 2007. DVD.

Bizzell, Patricia, and Bruce Herzberg. Introduction to *The Rhetorical Tradition: Readings from Classical Times to the Present,* 1–16. Boston: Bedford/St. Martin's, 2001.

Brandon, Lee. *At a Glance: Essays*. 3rd ed. Boston: Houghton Mifflin, 2006.

Brown, Stephen, Elizabeth Hirschman, and Pauline Maclaran. *Two Continents, One Culture*. Johnson City, TN: Overmountain Press, 2006.

Bullock, Richard. *The Norton Field Guide to Writing*. 2nd ed. New York: Norton, 2009.

Clapp, Elsie. *Community schools in action*. New York: Viking Press, 1939.

Clark, Amy D. "Family Matters: A Mother and Daughter's Literacy Journey." *National Writing Project*. Last modified November 2, 2009. https://www.nwp.org/cs/public/print/resource/2994.

———. "Letters from Home: The Literate Lives of Central Appalachian Women." *Appalachian Journal* 41, no. 1–2 (Fall 2013–Winter 2014): 54–76.

———. "Voices in the Appalachian Classroom." In *Talking Appalachian*, edited by Amy D. Clark and Nancy M. Hayward, 110–24. Lexington: University of Kentucky Press, 2013.

Clark, Amy D., and Nancy M. Hayward, ed. *Talking Appalachian: Voice, Identity, and Community*. Lexington: University of Kentucky Press, 2013.

Collins, Suzanne. *The Hunger Games*. New York: Scholastic, 2008.

Connell, Sarah. "Writing on the Land of Ireland: Nationality, Textuality, and Geography in the *Acallam na Senórach*." *Hortulus Journal* 7, no. 1 (2011): 5–30. Accessed September 10, 2017. https://hortulus-journal.com/journal/volume-7-number-1–2011/connell/.

Cooper, Marilyn M. "Rhetorical Agency as Emergent and Enacted." *CCC* 62, no. 3 (2011): 420–49.

Corbett, Edward P. J., and Robert J. Connors. *Classical Rhetoric for the Modern Student*. 4th ed. New York: Oxford University Press, 1990.

Dallas, Kelsey. "'Hillbilly Elegy': Best-Selling Author J.D. Vance on Faith in Appalachia." *Oakland Press*. Last modified September 14, 2016. http://www.theoaklandpress.com/lifestyle/20160914/hillbilly-elegy-best-selling-author-jd-vance-on-faith-in-appalachia.

Delpit, Lisa. "The Politics of Teaching Literate Discourse." In *Freedom's Plow: Teaching in the Multicultural Classroom*, edited by Theresa Perry and James W. Fraser, 285–96. New York: Routledge, 1993.

DeWitt, David. "Historian: Appalachia Has Record of Social Injustice." *Athens News* (Athens, Ohio). April 6, 2014.

DiYanni, Robert, and Pat C. Hoy, II. *Frames of Mind: A Rhetorical Reader with Occasions for Writing*. 2nd ed. Boston: Wadsworth Cengage Learning, 2009.

Donehower, Kim. "Rhetorics and Realities: The History and Effects of Stereotypes About Rural Literacies." In *Rural Literacies*, edited by Kim

Donehower, Charlotte Hogg, and Eileen E. Schell, 37–76. Carbondale, IL: Southern Illinois University Press, 2007.

Elbow, Peter. "Bringing the Rhetoric of Assent and the Believing Game Together—and into the Classroom." *College English* 67, no. 4 (2005): 388–99.

———. "Inviting the Mother Tongue: Beyond 'Mistakes,' 'Bad English,' and 'Wrong Language.'" *JAC* 19, no. 3 (1999): 359–88.

Fawcett, Susan. *Grassroots with Readings*. Boston: Houghton Mifflin, 2006.

Fisher, Diane Gilliam. Reading of *Kettle Bottom*. Athens, OH: Ohio University Press, 2012.

Flanigan, Beverly Olson. "Appalachian Women and Language: Old and New Forms as Reflections of a Changing Image." In *Beyond Hill and Hollow: Original Readings in Appalachian Women's Studies*, edited by Elizabeth S. D. Engelhardt, 177–97. Athens, OH: Ohio University Press, 2005.

Fleckenstein, Kristie S., Clay Spinuzzi, Rebecca J. Rickly, Carol Clark Papper. "The Importance of Harmony: An Ecological Metaphor for Writing Research." *CCC* 60, no. 2 (2008): 388–418.

Fox, Helen. *Listening to the World: Cultural Issues in Academic Writing*. Urbana, IL: NCTE, 1994.

Fulton, Helen. Introduction to *Medieval Celtic Literature and Society*, 11–14. Portland: Four Courts Press, 2005.

Gee, James Paul. "Literacy, Discourse, and Linguistics: Introduction." *Journal of Education* 171, no. 1 (1989): 5–17.

Gorski, Paul C. "Unlearning Deficit Ideology and the Scornful Gaze." In *Assault on Kids: How Hyper-Accountability, Corporatization, Deficit Ideologies, and Ruby Payne are Destroying Our Schools*, edited by Roberta Ahlquist, Paul Gorski, Theresa Montaño, 153–72. New York: Peter Lang, 2011.

Green, Emma. "It Was Cultural Anxiety That Drove White, Working-Class Voters to Trump." *Atlantic*. Last modified May 9, 2017. https://www.theatlantic.com/politics/archive/2017/05/white-working-class-trump-cultural-anxiety/525771/.

Hare, Heather. "OU Courses Examine Culture and Setbacks of Life in Appalachia." *Post* (Athens, Ohio). January 13, 2015.

Harper, Elsa Crooks. *An Enchanted Childhood at Raven Rocks*. Beallsville, OH: Raven Rocks Press, 1986.

Harris, Joseph. "The Idea of Community in the Study of Writing." *CCC* 40, no. 1 (1989): 11–22.

"Hate Map." *Southern Poverty Law Center*. Accessed August 10, 2014. https://www.splcenter.org/hate-map.

Heath, Shirley Brice. *Ways with Words: Language, Life, and Work in Communities and Classrooms*. Cambridge: Cambridge University Press, 1983.

Hofstra, Warren R., ed. Introduction to *Ulster to America: The Scots-Irish Migration Experience, 1680–1830*. Knoxville: University of Tennessee Press, 2012.

Holloway, Kimberley M, ed. *From a Race of Storytellers: The Ballad Novels of Sharyn McCrumb*. Macon, GA: Mercer University Press, 2003.

Horner, Bruce, and John Trimbur. "English Only and U.S. College Composition." *CCC* 53, no. 4 (2002): 594–630.

Hutton, Bob. "Hillbilly Elitism." *Jacobin*. Accessed October 1, 2016. https://www.jacobinmag.com/2016/10/hillbilly-elegy-review-jd-vance-national-review-white-working-class-appalachia/.

Iddings, Joshua, and Ryan Angus. "A Functional Linguistics Approach to Appalachian Literacies." In *Re-Reading Appalachia*, edited by Sara Webb-Sunderhaus and Kim Donehower, 157–78. Lexington: University of Kentucky Press, 2015.

Jackson, Stevan R. "Peoples of Appalachia: Cultural Diversity within the Mountain Region." In *A Handbook to Appalachia: An Introduction to the Region*, edited by Grace Toney Edwards, JoAnn Aust Asbury, and Ricky L. Cox, 27–49. Knoxville: University of Tennessee Press, 2006.

Johnson-Sheehan, Richard, and Paul Lynch. "Rhetoric of Myth, Magic, and Conversion: A Prolegomena to Ancient Irish Rhetoric." *Rhetoric Review* 26, no. 3 (2007): 233–52.

Jones, Loyal. *Appalachian Values*. Ashland, NC: The Jesse Stewart Foundation, 1994.

Joyce, Rosemary Owsley. "A Woman's Place: The Life History of a Rural Ohio Grandmother." Ph.D. diss., The Ohio State University, 1980.

Keown-Bomar, Julie, and Deborah Patee. "What's Class Got to Do with It?" In *Assault on Kids: How Hyper-Accountability, Corporatization, Deficit Ideologies, and Ruby Payne are Destroying Our Schools*, edited by Roberta Ahlquist, Paul Gorski, and Theresa Montaño, 214–36. New York: Peter Lang, 2011.

Kindness, Della Grace. *The Way It Was*. Antrim, OH: printed by the author, 2003.

Kirk, Gwyn, and Margo Okazawa-Rey. *Women's Lives: Multicultural Perspectives*. 6th ed. Boston: McGraw-Hill, 2012.

Lewis, Helen. "The Colony of Appalachia." In *Colonialism in Modern America: The Appalachian Case*, edited by Helen Lewis, Linda Johnson, and Donald Askins, 1–5. Boone, NC: Appalachian Consortium Press, 1978.

Lindgren, Tim. "Blogging Places: Locating Pedagogy in the Whereness of Weblogs." *Kairos* 10, no. 1 (2005). Accessed September 10, 2017. http://english.ttu.edu/kairos/10.1/binder2.html?coverweb/lindgren/index.htm.

Locklear, Erica Abrams. "Narrating Socialization: Linda Scott DeRosier's Memoirs." *Community Literacy Journal* 2, no. 1 (2007): 41–57.

Lynch, Paul. "'Ego Patricius, Peccator Rusticissimus': The Rhetoric of St. Patrick of Ireland." *Rhetoric Review* 27, no. 2 (2008): 111–30.

Lynn, Loretta. *Coal Miner's Daughter.* New York: Vintage, 2010.

Lyons, Scott Richard. "Rhetorical Sovereignty: What Do American Indians Want from Writing?" *CCC* 51, no. 3 (2000): 447–570.

Madden, David. *A Pocketful of Essays Volume 1: Rhetorically Arranged.* Fort Worth: Harcourt College Publishers, 2001.

Marshall, Peter. *Nature's Web: Rethinking Our Place on Earth.* New York: Paragon House, 1992.

Mathieu, Paula, Tim Lindgren, George Grattan, and Staci Shultz. *Writing Places.* New York: Pearson Longman, 2006.

McCrumb, Sharyn. *Sharyn McCrumb's Appalachia: A Collection of Essays on the Mountain South.* Waverly, TN: Oconee Spirit Press, 2011.

———. *The Songcatcher.* New York: Signet, 2001.

Minor, Dorothy, ed. *Patterns: A Prentice Hall Pocket Reader.* Upper Saddle River, NJ: Pearson Prentice Hall, 2005.

Montano, Theresa, and Rosalinda Quintanar-Sarellana. "Undoing Ruby Payne and Other Deficit Views of English Language Learners." In *Assault on Kids: How Hyper-Accountability, Corporatization, Deficit Ideologies, and Ruby Payne Are Destroying Our Schools*, edited by Roberta Ahlquist, Paul Gorski, Theresa Montaño, 199–213. New York: Peter Lang, 2011.

Montgomery, Michael. "The Historical Background and Nature of the Englishes of Appalachia." In *Talking Appalachian*, edited by Amy D. Clark and Nancy M. Hayward, 25–53. Lexington: University of Kentucky Press, 2013.

———. "How Scotch-Irish Is Your English? The Ulster Heritage of East Tennessee Speech." *The Ulster-Scots Language Society.* Accessed July 19, 2010. http://www.ulsterscotslanguage.com/en/texts/scotch-irish/how-scotch-irish-is-your-english/.

———. "Language." In *Encyclopedia of Appalachia*, edited by Rudy Abramson and Jean Haskell, 999–1005. Knoxville: University of Tennessee Press, 2006.

Mountain Talk. Directed by Neal Hutcheson. Raleigh, NC: NCLLP Films, 2004. DVD.

O' Driscoll, Robert. *The Celtic Consciousness*. New York: George Braziller, Inc, 1981.

"Ohio Social Studies Standards." *Ohio Department of Education*. Accessed June, 2010. https://education.ohio.gov/getattachment/Topics/Ohio-s-New-Learning-Standards/Social-Studies/SS-Standards.pdf.aspx.

O' Riordan, Michelle. *The Gaelic Mind and the Collapse of the Gaelic World*. Cork: Cork University Press, 1990.

O' Snodaigh, Padraig. *Hidden Ulster: Protestants and the Irish Language*. Belfast: Lagan Press, 1995.

Patterson, Daniel W. *The True Image: Gravestone Art and The Culture of Scotch Irish Settlers in the Pennsylvania and Carolina Backcountry*. Chapel Hill, NC: University of North Carolina Press, 2012.

Patterson, Nerys. *Cattle Lords and Clansmen: The Social Structure of Early Ireland*. London: University of Notre Dame Press, 1994.

Payne, Ruby. *A Framework for Understanding Poverty*. 3rd ed. Highlands, TX: Aha! Process, Inc., 1996.

Penix, Amanda Griffith. *Arthurdale*. Charleston: Arcadia Press, 2007.

Pryce, Huw, ed. *Literacy in Medieval Celtic Societies*. Cambridge: Cambridge University Press, 1998.

Purcell-Gates, Victoria. "' . . . As Soon as She Opened Her Mouth!': Issues of Language, Literacy, and Power." In *The Skin That We Speak: Thoughts on Language and Culture in the Classroom*, edited by Lisa Delpit and Joanne Kilgour Dowdy, 121–44. New York: The New Press, 2002.

Reaser, Jeffrey. "Dialect and Education in Appalachia." In *Talking Appalachian*, edited by Amy D. Clark and Nancy M. Hayward, 94–109. Lexington: University of Kentucky Press, 2013.

Redeaux, Monique. "A Framework for Maintaining White Privilege: A Critique of Ruby Payne." In *Assault on Kids: How Hyper-Accountability, Corporatization, Deficit Ideologies, and Ruby Payne are Destroying Our Schools*, edited by Roberta Ahlquist, Paul Gorski, and Theresa Montaño, 177–98. New York: Peter Lang, 2011.

Ritchie, Joy, and Kate Ronald. Introduction to *Available Means: An Anthology of Women's Rhetoric(s)*, xv–xxi. Pittsburgh: University of Pittsburgh Press, 2001.

Roth-Howe, Deborah, Herbert L. Roth, Gabrielle Schmitt, Annegret Wenz-Haubfleish, and Rabbi Robert Sternberg. "An Unlikely Alliance: Germans and Jews Collaborate to Teach the Lessons of the Holocaust." In *Telling Stories to Change the World*, edited by Rickie Solinger, Madeline Fox, and Kayhan Irani, 55–64. New York: Routledge, 2008.

Sanchez, Deborah M., and Eric J. Paulson. "Critical Language Awareness and Learners in College Transitional English." *Teaching English in the Two-Year College* 36, no. 2 (2008): 164–76.

Satlin, Alana Horowitz, and Sam Levine. "White House Budget Director Says Single Moms Shouldn't Have to Pay for PBS." *Huffington Post.* Last modified March 16, 2017. http://www.huffingtonpost.com/entry/white-house-budget-sesame-street-pbs_us_58ca8cade4b0be71dcf1d3eb.

Scherman, Katharine. *The Flowering of Ireland: Saints, Scholars, and Kings.* Boston: Little, Brown, and Company, 1981.

Shepley, Nathan. "Places of Composition: Writing Contexts in Appalachian Ohio." *Composition Studies* 37, no. 2 (2009): 75–90.

Smith, Lee. "Southern Exposure." In *Talking Appalachian*, edited by Amy D. Clark and Nancy M. Hayward, 205–08. Lexington: University of Kentucky Press, 2013.

Smitherman, Geneva. *Talkin That Talk: Language, Culture, and Education in African America.* London: Routledge, 1999.

Snyder, Todd. *The Rhetoric of Appalachian Identity.* Jefferson, NC: McFarland and Company, Inc, 2014.

Sohn, Katherine Kelleher. "Silence, Voice, and Identity among Appalachian College Women." In *Talking Appalachian*, edited by Amy D. Clark and Nancy M. Hayward, 125–40. Lexington: University of Kentucky Press, 2013.

———. *Whistlin' and Crowin' Women of Appalachia: Literacy Practices since College.* Carbondale, IL: Southern Illinois University Press, 2006.

Smith, Lee. "Southern Exposure." In *Talking Appalachian*, edited by Amy D. Clark and Nancy M. Hayward, 205–08. Lexington: University of Kentucky Press, 2013.

Spring, Joel. *The American School.* 5th ed. Boston: McGraw-Hill, 2001.

Stacey, Robin Chapman. "Law and Literature in Medieval Ireland and Wales." In *Medieval Celtic Literature and Society*, edited by Helen Fulton, 65–82. Dublin: Four Courts Press, 2005.

Stephen Fry In America. Directed by John-Paul Davidson and Michael Waldman. London: Sprout Pictures, 2008. DVD.

Teets, Sharon. "Education in Appalachia." In *A Handbook to Appalachia*, edited by Grace Toney Edwards, JoAnne Aust Asbury, and Ricky L. Cox, 119–42. Knoxville: University of Tennessee Press, 2006.

Theobald, Paul. *Education Now: How Rethinking America's Past Can Change Its Future.* Boulder: Paradigm Publishers, 2009.

Thompson, Deborah, and Irene Moser. "Appalachian Folklife." In *A Handbook to Appalachia: An Introduction to the Region*, edited by Grace

Toney Edwards, JoAnne Aust Asbury, and Ricky L. Cox, 143–62. Knoxville: University of Tennessee Press, 2006.

Toobin, Jeffrey. "What's the Matter with West Virginia?" *New Yorker*. Last modified November 19, 2014. http://www.newyorker.com/news/daily-comment/whats-matter-west-virginia.

Trigiani, Adriana. "The Origin Project." Accessed September 9, 2017. http://adrianatrigiani.com/the-origin-project/.

Valentine, Fawn. *West Virginia Quilts and Quiltmakers: Echoes from the Hills*. Athens, OH: Ohio University Press, 2000.

Vance, J.D. *Hillbilly Elegy: A Memoir of a Family and Culture in Crisis*. New York: HarperCollins, 2016.

Villanueva, Victor. Foreword to *Whistlin' and Crowin' Women of Appalachia: Literacy Practices since College*, by Katherine Kelleher Sohn, xiii–xv. Carbondale, IL: Southern Illinois University Press, 2006.

Webb-Sunderhaus, Sara. "A Family Affair: Competing Sponsors of Literacy in Appalachian Students' Lives." *Community Literacy Journal* 2, no. 1 (2007): 5–24.

Webb-Sunderhaus, Sara, and Kim Donehower, eds. *Re-Reading Appalachia: Literacy, Place, and Cultural Resistance*. Lexington: University of Kentucky Press, 2015.

Wheeler, Rebecca, and Rachel Swords. *Code-Switching Lessons: Grammar Strategies for Linguistically Diverse Writers*. Portsmouth, NH: Firsthand Heinemann, 2010.

Whited, Lana. "Review: The Hunger Games." *Journal of Appalachian Studies* 18, no. 1 (2012): 326–31.

Wigginton, Eliot. Introduction to *The Foxfire Book*, 9–16. New York: Anchor, 1972.

Wilder, Laura Ingalls. *Little House in the Big Woods*. New York: Harper & Brothers, 1932.

Williams, Patricia. *The Alchemy of Race and Rights: Diary of a Law Professor*. Cambridge, MA: Harvard University Press, 1991.

Index